Plagues

Titles in the Natural Disasters series include:

Natural **Disasters**

Plagues

by Kris Hirschmann

Lucent Books
San Diego, California

Library of Congress Cataloging-in-Publication Data

Hirschmann, Kris, 1967–
     Plagues / by Kris Hirschmann.
        p. cm. — (Natural disasters)
     Includes bibliographical references and index.
     Summary: Defines and discusses certain calamitous
events around the world, from past to modern times, that
have resulted in death, famine, or economic destruction.
     ISBN 1-56006-976-7 (alk. paper)
     1. Epidemics. [1. Epidemics. 2. Animal introduction. 3.
Plant invasions.] I. Title. II. Natural disasters (Lucent Books)
     RA653.5 .H55 2002
     614.4'9—dc21

                                                2001003012

Copyright © 2002 by Lucent Books, Inc.
10911 Technology Place, San Diego, CA 92127
Printed in the U.S.A.

Contents

Foreword

Fear and fascination are the two most common human responses to nature's most devastating events. People fear the awesome force of an earthquake, a volcanic eruption, a hurricane, and other natural phenomena with good reason. An earthquake can reduce multistory buildings to rubble in a matter of seconds. A volcanic eruption can turn lush forests and glistening lakes into a gray, flat landscape of mud and ash. A hurricane can lift houses from their foundations and hurl trucks and steel beams through the air.

As one witness to Hurricane Andrew, which hit Florida in 1992, recounts: "After the storm, planks and pieces of plywood were found impaling the trunks of large palms. . . . Eighteen-foot-long steel and concrete tie beams with roofs still attached were carried more than 150 feet. Paint was peeled from walls and street signs were sucked out of the ground and hurled through houses. Flying diesel fuel drums were a hazard, as were signs, awnings, decks, trash barrels, and fence posts that filled the skies. Mobile homes not only blew apart during the storm but disintegrated into aluminum shrapnel that became embedded in surrounding structures."

Fear is an understandable response to an event such as this but it is not the only emotion people experience when caught in the throes of a natural disaster or when news of one blares from radios or flashes across television screens. Most people are fascinated by natural forces that have the power to claim life, crush homes, tear trees from their roots, and devastate whole communities—all in an instant. Why do such terrible events as these fascinate people? Perhaps the answer lies in humanity's inability to control them, and in the knowledge that they will recur—in some cases without warning—despite the scientific community's best efforts to understand and predict them.

A great deal of scientific study has been devoted to understanding and predicting natural phenomena such as earthquakes, volcanic eruptions, and hurricanes. Geologists and seismologists monitor the earth's motion from thousands of locations around the world. Their sensitive instruments record even the slightest shifts in the large tectonic plates that make up the earth's crust. Tools such as these have greatly improved efforts to predict natural disasters. When Mt. Pinatubo in the Philippines awoke from its six-hundred-year slumber in 1991, for example, a team of scientists armed with seismometers, tiltmeters, and personal computers successfully predicted when the volcano would explode.

Clearly, the scientific community has made great strides in knowledge and in the ability to monitor and even predict some of nature's most catastrophic events. Prediction techniques have not yet been perfected, however, and control of these events eludes humanity entirely. From the moment a tropical disturbance forms over the ocean, for example, researchers can track its progress and follow every twist in its path to becoming a hurricane but they cannot predict with certainty where it will make landfall. As one researcher writes: "No one knows when or where [a catastrophic hurricane] will strike, but we do know that eventually it will blast ashore somewhere and cause massive destruction. . . . Since there is nothing anyone can do to alter that foreboding reality, the question is: Are we ready for the next great hurricane?"

The many gaps in knowledge, coupled with the inability to control these events and the certainty that they will recur, may help explain humanity's continuing fascination with natural disasters. The Natural Disasters series provides clear and careful explanations, vivid examples, and the latest information about how and why these events occur, as well as what efforts are being made to predict them and to prepare for them. Annotated bibliographies provide readers with ideas for further research. Fully documented primary and secondary source quotations enliven the text. Each book in this series provides students with a wealth of information as well as launching points for further study.

Introduction

From the Hand
of God?

The word "plague" means different things to different people. To a medical professional, it conjures visions of gruesome diseases. To a farmer, it may represent disastrous crop blights that lead to financial ruin and, perhaps, starvation. To a government agency, it may mean plant and animal invaders intent on destroying a country's natural resources. And to residents of rural Africa and other insect-ravaged parts of the world, the word may signify an especially elemental horror: clouds of crawling, chewing locusts that descend thickly and without warning from a clear blue sky, devour every scrap of vegetation they can find, and then move on, leaving barren fields in their wake.

No matter what form it takes, a plague by its very definition is calamitous, generally bringing death, famine, or economic destruction. Under the most favorable circumstances, a plague may impact merely thousands of people. A severe plague, however, can affect millions, perhaps even changing the course of human history in the process. It is no wonder, then, that people through the ages have dreaded the coming of a plague.

Intentional Afflictions

That dread has always been amplified by uncertainty. What type of plague would come next? Where and when would it strike? And when it did strike, how bad would it be? It was impossible to even guess at the answers to these questions hundreds of years ago, when humankind had not yet identified things like the pathogens that cause disease, the fungi that turn crops into rotting mush, and the natural cycles of locust swarms. To the afflicted, it often seemed that plagues arrived without warning or cause, flung to earth by the very hand of God.

Evidence of this view is actually embedded in the language. The modern word "plague" is a descendant of the Latin *plaga*, which means a blow or wound. The word *plaga* in turn is related to the Latin *plangere*, which means to strike. The act of striking implies one who strikes and one who is struck. Thus the very roots of the word "plague" suggest that such events have historically been regarded as blows intentionally inflicted on weak or erring humans by an all-powerful and perhaps angry deity.

Targeted Torment

It is not hard to understand why people might have felt that plagues had been sent to them deliberately. Epidemics, blights, and other plague afflictions seem somehow targeted, perhaps more so than other types of natural disasters. Forces such as tornadoes, earthquakes, and hurricanes are frightening and damaging, but they are

Throughout history plagues have killed thousands and sometimes even millions of people. Until recently, people believed that these plagues were sent to them deliberately as punishment from God.

also impersonal. A tornado smashes everything, human or otherwise, in its path. An earthquake shakes the ground whether or not people are nearby. A hurricane destroys homes, but it also uproots trees, kills woodland animals, and generally wreaks havoc on all things equally.

Now consider the case of plagues, which seem to be designed especially to cause human misery. A deadly disease may strike people, for example, but bypass a town's animal inhabitants. Essential human food crops may fail while weeds and flowers flourish in the very same field. Marauding insects may infest human homes exclusively, ignoring other seemingly suitable spots. It is no wonder that people through the ages have viewed plagues as personal attacks.

This is, of course, a one-sided perspective. Every species on earth is subject to its own plagues; nothing is immune. But people tend to focus most on issues that affect them directly. It is probably human nature to take misfortune personally, especially when the causes of that misfortune are not evident.

The Modern View

Today, many of the causes of plagues *are* evident. Modern scientific technology has enabled humans to study bacteria, viruses, and other microscopic disease agents. Global connectivity makes it easy to track the spread of invasive alien species from one country to another. The relationships between fungal pathogens (certain types of fungi) and food crops are well documented; the seasonal and climatic patterns that encourage swarms of insects and other animals are both understood and predictable.

This knowledge explosion has given birth to a new attitude about plagues. For the first time in history, humans do not feel completely helpless in the face of these old enemies. Instead, they feel empowered to fight back—and they are doing so with a vengeance. Governments and scientists are forever seeking new ways to conquer the plagues that continue to pop up around the world. Although absolute victory is rare, modern techniques can often minimize a plague's consequences. The battle therefore can be both worthy and rewarding.

USDA technicians conduct a field experiment in an effort to control an epidemic of lesser peach tree borers. Modern scientific technology has provided scientists with the tools to study the agents that cause plagues, and to find ways to conquer them.

So humankind has achieved some measure of control over once impossible circumstances. This feeling of control, however, may carry its own dangers. A plague, after all, is a slippery thing that arrives unexpectedly and hits hardest where people are weakest. Humankind can ill afford to relax its vigilance against the known killers—or drop its guard against new ones. And how will those new plagues show themselves? Where and when will they strike? How bad will they be when they do?

Across the centuries, the questions have remained much the same.

Pestilence

Pestilence is the most terrifying of all plagues, in part because it is invisible to the human eye. The viruses and bacteria that cause infectious diseases are far too tiny to be seen, which means that they can strike anywhere, anytime, without being noticed. Even worse, they attack from within the body, bringing a foul death that strips the sufferer of dignity and humanity. The survivors suffer, too: They must endure not only grief at the passing of their loved ones, but also the fear that they will be next.

Most infectious diseases do not present a major threat to humankind. Some simply are not very dangerous. A person is likely to survive dozens of colds during the course of a lifetime as well as a handful of more serious ailments such as influenza, chicken pox, and strep throat. Other diseases, such as Ebola hemorrhagic fever, are extremely dangerous, but can be fairly easily contained if the proper precautions are taken. They are also quickly identified. Such illnesses therefore can usually be stopped before they infect too many people.

A handful of diseases, however, are both deadly and difficult to contain. When one of these diseases breaks into the human population, an epidemic (defined as an infectious disease that strikes a large number of people at the same time) may erupt. Major epidemics are thankfully rare—but when they occur, their effects can be severe enough to change the very course of history.

Spread of the Black Death

One of the most disastrous epidemics in human history struck Europe in the mid-1300s. Author James Cross Giblin describes the symptoms of the disease:

Its victims suffered from headaches, felt weak and tired, and staggered when they tried to walk. By the third day, the lymph nodes in the sufferers' groins, or occasionally their armpits, began to swell. Soon they reached the size of hens' eggs. . . . The victim's heart beat wildly as it tried to pump blood through the swollen tissues. The nervous system started to collapse, causing dreadful pain and bizarre movements of the arms and legs. Then, as death neared, the mouth gaped open and the skin blackened from internal bleeding. The end usually came on the fifth day.[1]

The characteristic blackening of the skin gave the disease its name: the Black Death. It is also known as the bubonic plague, or simply the plague.

Bubonic plague was known in China as early as A.D. 46, but it was confined to remote Chinese steppes for centuries. In the early 1300s, however, expanding world trade enabled the disease to move westward. It traveled unnoticed on wagons and ships inside fleas, whose tiny bodies served as vessels for plague-causing bacteria. These fleas lived on the backs of common black rats, which could easily slip from ship to shore in a new land.

Pictured is a bubonic plague victim during the Middle Ages. Victims of the deadly disease usually perished within just five days.

The Plague Strikes

The first plague-bearing rats arrived in Sicily (an island off the coast of Italy) in 1347. They found living conditions there very much to their liking—that is to say, crowded and filthy. The rats moved into people's homes, bringing their lethal fleas with them. In such close quarters, it was inevitable that the fleas would soon find their way onto human bodies. Poor sanitation also played its part, explains author James Cross Giblin: "Because the cities had no running water, even the wealthy seldom washed their heavy clothing, or their own bodies. As a result, both rich and poor were prime targets for fleas and the diseases they carried."[2]

The results were deadly. The plague rolled across Sicily in a great wave, killing as it went. The disease soon spread to Italy, then to France, Spain, and Germany. By 1349 the plague had leaped across the sea and landed in England.

Wherever the plague appeared, death appeared as well. Corpses became so numerous that officials were forced to collect them with "death carts" and then dump them unceremoniously into mass graves. Agnolo di Tura, a resident of Siena, Italy, wrote this harrowing description of conditions at the height of the plague:

> Great pits were dug and piled deep with the multitude of the dead. And they died by the hundreds, both day and night, and all were thrown in those ditches and covered with earth. And as soon as those ditches were filled, more were dug. I, Agnolo di Tura . . . buried my five children with my own hands. . . . And so many died that all believed it was the end of the world.[3]

The healthy population reacted to the scourge in various ways. Some people fled the cities. Many refused to get anywhere near the corpses of plague victims, with the result that bodies piled up inside homes and on the streets. And some people simply shrugged their shoulders and abandoned themselves to the will of God. "They drank heavily, stayed out late, and roamed through the streets singing and dancing as if the Black Death were an enormous joke,"[4] writes James Cross Giblin.

Efforts to Subdue the Killer

Medical professionals were baffled. They had no idea what was causing the plague, how to treat it, or how to bring it under control. But they tried. The most common action was strict quarantine. In the city-state of Venice, for example, incoming ships were observed for forty days before being permitted to land. This policy proved ineffective, of course, because it did not apply to the rats. Although sailors stayed aboard their ships, the rats came and went as they pleased.

In other areas, plague victims were confined to their homes to keep them away from the population at large. Healthy family members were shut in, too—"a virtual death sentence for all within the household,"[5] explains historian Ron Wild. But even these drastic measures failed. For although plague homes were being isolated, the real problem—the rats—was not.

As official efforts failed, folk remedies started to appear. Many people believed that the Black Death traveled through the air—perhaps, as Boise State University history professor E. L. Skip Knox speculates, "because the smell from the dead and

Incense is burned to ward off the sickening stench coming from the corpses and victims dying of the Black Death.

dying was so awful."[6] Incense burned constantly, and those who were forced to venture outside held scented handkerchiefs over their noses and mouths to ward off the plague. Loud noises were another trusted remedy; church bells pealed at all hours and cannons were fired in an effort to drive away the disease.

The Black Death finally subsided of its own accord in 1352, probably because it had run out of vulnerable targets. The final death count was staggering. Within five years the plague had taken the lives of approximately 25 million people, or about one-third of the population of Europe. And the killer was not even gone for good. It would strike Europe again and again until the late 1600s, sometimes claiming hundreds of thousands of lives during an outbreak.

No Resistance

Why was the Black Death able to wreak such havoc? It was mostly because Europe's population had never before been exposed to the disease. Over time, the human body builds up defenses against common ailments. But the body cannot defend itself against a disease it has never known. So when an illness moves into a previously untouched pool of people, there is nothing to stop it from exploding.

Even in "virgin" populations, however, some people are naturally resistant to certain new diseases. Susceptible people die in droves, but those who are resistant survive and develop antibodies (disease-fighting agents) against the disease. At the same time, the disease mutates and grows weaker over time. Eventually human and plague settle into an uneasy truce: The disease agents are present all the time, but they must remain dormant until a new pool of prey appears. When this balance is reached, a disease is said to be endemic.

History has shown again and again what happens when one culture's endemic disease is carried into a virgin population. One dramatic example occurred in the 1500s, when European explorers brought smallpox to the regions now known as Central America and South America. The disease tore through the mighty Inca and Aztec civilizations, reducing them to a fraction of their former size and handing Europe an easy conquest of the region.

A Close Call

In 1997 a new strain of influenza was identified in Hong Kong. Dubbed H5N1, the virus affected only chickens at first. But then people started catching the bug—and it became clear that the world's human population was in grave danger. In her *Discover* magazine article "Fear of Flu," author Patricia Gadsby describes the pandemic that almost was.

In May 1997 [the virus] killed its first human victim, a three-year-old boy whose preschool had kept little chicks and ducklings. Now, with winter setting in, this fluky virus was breaking out in humans again—four cases were confirmed in November, thirteen in December. More alarming still, a third of the victims were dying.

As long as H5N1 remained [a] bird virus, its opportunities for infecting people were limited. But what if H5N1 mutated into a form more at home in humans? Or what if it joined in unholy matrimony with a human flu virus and created viral offspring that spread easily—flying from person to person through coughs and sneezes? "This had never happened before in history," says [virologist Kennedy] Shortridge. "It was terrifying."

On December 29, the government grimly went ahead with the slaughter of all the chickens in the markets and farms, well over a million birds. Chinese New Year came and went, celebrated without the traditional fresh poultry dishes. No more human H5N1 cases. Months went by. The crisis in Hong Kong began to seem less like a close call than an overreaction. Robert Webster, a virologist at St. Jude Children's Research Hospital in Memphis, completely disagrees. "If this virus had really adapted to humans," he says, "half the world's population could be dead by now. We'd be looking at the next pandemic."

For now, researchers are catching their breath, immensely relieved that H5N1 was nipped in the bud. But Webster feels that another hop from birds to humans will occur in the near future. The Hong Kong outbreak, he adds, "served as a warning of what could happen. It was a killer—like 1918 on its way."

Smallpox and other epidemics took an even greater toll on the areas now known as the United States and Canada. Historians estimate that European-introduced diseases killed as much as 90 percent of the Native American population over the course of four centuries.

The Spanish Flu Pandemic of 1918

The spread of a known disease is bad enough—but the story doesn't end there. Bacteria and viruses have the ability to mutate over time. Most of the time these mutations are harmless. Every now and then, however, they create new diseases that can rip an unprepared population to shreds.

Such was the case as recently as 1918, when a previously unknown strain of influenza (the flu) burst onto the world scene. It started quietly enough: A soldier at Fort Riley in Kansas entered the camp's infirmary complaining of a "bad cold." That "bad cold" turned out to be the first recorded case of an incredibly contagious new disease. The illness spread through the air, which meant that a few hearty sneezes or coughs from a flu victim could contaminate an entire room. By lunchtime more than one hundred soldiers had been admitted to the Fort Riley infirmary.

Within weeks the disease (which came to be known as the Spanish flu) had exploded out of Fort Riley and around the world, where it embarked on a killing spree the likes of which mankind had not seen for centuries. Although the pandemic (worldwide epidemic) ran its course in nine short months, its effects were devastating. In the United States alone, nearly seven hundred thousand people died from the disease. That figure exceeds the number of American soldiers killed during World War I, World War II, the Korean War, and the Vietnam War *combined*. Worldwide the death toll exceeded 20 million—a number then equal to approximately one in every one hundred people in the entire world.

Daily Death

Luckily for humankind, major outbreaks on the scale of the Black Death and the Spanish flu are relatively rare. Pestilence in general, however, is not. According to the World Health

Children and adults wait in line for flu inoculations during the Spanish flu outbreak of 1918, which killed more than 20 million people worldwide.

Organization (WHO), 63 percent of all childhood deaths and 48 percent of all premature deaths are caused even today by infectious diseases.

Wealthy countries whose citizens enjoy clean, uncrowded living conditions seldom experience major outbreaks. But poor people in underdeveloped countries live with the daily fear of infectious disease. Filth-loving ailments such as cholera and dysentery are constant threats in unsanitary areas; outbreaks of such diseases claim millions of lives each year. Childhood illnesses such as measles and whooping cough take their toll around the world. Other traditional enemies of humankind that are endemic in many areas today include tetanus, hepatitis, meningitis, yellow fever, dengue fever, and leprosy, to name just a few.

Tuberculosis (TB), a longtime human enemy, stands out as a particular threat. This highly contagious respiratory disease runs rampant in sub-Saharan Africa and Southeast Asia. According to the WHO, TB infects 8 million people each year. Of those, 2 to

3 million die. And the situation is not getting any better: "It is estimated that between 2000 and 2020, nearly one billion people will be newly infected, 200 million people will get sick, and 35 million will die from TB if control is not further strengthened,"[7] according to the WHO.

Medical Pioneers

The fact that control is even possible is a major step forward for humankind. As recently as two hundred years ago doctors had no idea what caused diseases. They could not prevent them, and they certainly had no effective drugs with which to treat them. But that situation has changed dramatically thanks to the efforts of a few brilliant scientists.

The first breakthrough came in 1796, when British scientist Edward Jenner developed a safe, effective vaccine against smallpox. No one knew exactly why or how the vaccine worked; they

Edward Jenner vaccinates a small child against smallpox. Jenner's vaccination, which he developed in 1796, was the first major breakthrough in disease prevention.

only knew that it did. For the first time in history, humans had the ability to stop a deadly disease from striking.

French chemist and biologist Louis Pasteur made another major advance in the mid-1800s with his germ theory. This theory stated that all diseases were caused by germs that entered the body from the outside, then attacked from within. The idea seems obvious today. At the time, however, it was met with open disbelief. "The notion that tiny organisms could kill vastly larger ones seemed ridiculous to many people,"[8] explains author Randy Bird.

Still, Pasteur was sure that he was right. His confidence was rewarded in the 1870s, when German scientist Robert Koch isolated the bacterium that causes anthrax. Koch's accomplishment proved beyond a doubt that at least *one* disease was caused by a specific germ. From that point on, the scientific community began to rally around Pasteur's germ theory, which eventually gained full acceptance.

Another medical advance of critical importance occurred in 1928, when British bacteriologist Alexander Fleming discovered that the mold called *Penicillium notatum* could kill bacteria. Fleming's discovery led to the development of penicillin, a drug that would revolutionize the field of medical care.

Cures . . . and Prevention

Today, penicillin and its relatives (known collectively as antibiotics) are essential weapons in the worldwide war on disease. Many dangerous bacterial ailments, including bubonic plague, diphtheria, syphilis, and typhoid, are highly susceptible to antibiotics. A patient suffering from one of these diseases is likely to survive if medicine is received quickly. This is a vast improvement over the pre-antibiotic era, when disease victims were often maimed, driven mad, or even killed by illnesses that can now be brought under control by taking a few little pills.

Viral diseases such as influenza, measles, polio, and hepatitis are more difficult to cure through the use of drugs. But scientists now understand the way viruses work and spread. This knowledge helps doctors prescribe effective treatments for people with viral diseases. It also allows medical workers to keep themselves safe

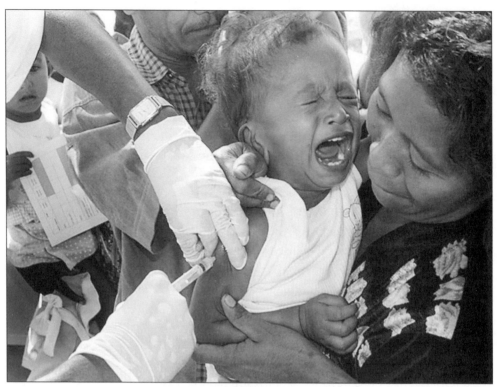

An East Timorese baby receives an inoculation for measles. Global vaccination programs run by the World Health Organization (WHO) have greatly reduced child mortality.

when they care for infected patients, which in turn helps stop the spread of disease.

The most important advance against disease, however, has been in the prevention rather than the cure. Governments and organizations around the world have established disease prevention programs, with childhood vaccination being the cornerstone of this effort. For several decades the WHO has directed an ambitious global immunization program designed to make people immune to many common diseases. The result, says the WHO, is that "child mortality has been greatly reduced, from 134 per 1,000 live births in 1970 to about 80 in 1995."[9] The program's most remarkable success has been the elimination of smallpox. Once a worldwide scourge, this disease has been wiped off the face of the earth through vaccination programs. Other diseases, including polio and measles, are close to being eradicated.

Many dangerous diseases still exist. But for those who do fall ill, improved health care and sanitation standards have greatly increased the chances of survival.

Entering the AIDS Era

Despite its many advances, medical science doesn't have all the answers. Scientists learned this lesson the hard way in the early 1980s when an unidentified disease started appearing in North America. The victims were mostly young, otherwise healthy men. The mysterious illness announced its presence through symptoms that included fatigue, coughing, fever, and rashes. More serious symptoms, such as unexplained weight loss, pneumonia, cancers, and fungal infections eventually developed. Death was the inevitable result.

Within a few years scientists had discovered the cause of the previously unseen disease. The culprit is a virus called HIV that is transmitted through the exchange of bodily fluids, including blood, semen, and breast milk. Sexual contact, intravenous drug use, and blood transfusions all can spread the virus; pregnant women who are HIV-positive can also pass the virus to their unborn babies.

HIV works by damaging a person's immune system over the course of several years. Eventually the body's natural defenses against harmful bacteria and viruses fail. When this stage is reached, the patient starts to fall ill with one disease after another. This acute stage of the illness is named AIDS, an acronym for Acquired Immune Deficiency Syndrome.

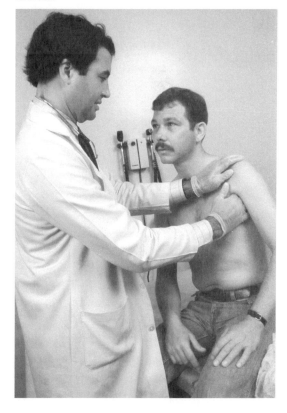

A doctor examines an AIDS patient in 1983. AIDS has claimed the lives of 21.8 million people in the past two decades.

The initial medical response to the AIDS threat was optimistic. "While there was no known cure for AIDS, fewer than one hundred thousand cases had been reported worldwide [by 1988]. In addition, the main methods of AIDS transmission were known. Surely, predictions of a new 'Black Death' were overblown,"[10] say authors Brent Hoff and Carter Smith III. But reality soon hit.

What the optimists had not counted on was that AIDS was like no disease ever faced before. AIDS is a slow killer, typically taking eight to ten years to claim its victims. This long incubation period would dramatically aid the spread of infection. What is more, HIV . . . has confounded researchers with its ability to adapt, changing genetically to protect itself against each new form of treatment.[11]

In short, the new disease appeared to be incurable. It was spreading like wildfire, and people were dying. AIDS was turning out to be a true plague indeed.

AIDS Today

Scant years later, that plague has grown to staggering proportions. UNAIDS, a global organization created to monitor the disease, reports that more than 36 million people were HIV-positive by the end of the year 2000. Total AIDS-related deaths since 1981 numbered 21.8 million at the end of the same year. Of those deaths, 3 million occurred during 2000 alone, making AIDS humankind's number-one infectious killer. And there is no sign of a letup. The world's AIDS epidemic is raging out of control and getting worse every year.

AIDS control, therefore, is one of the world's top health priorities, and public education is the first step in the control process. UNAIDS and other organizations have mounted worldwide campaigns to teach people how to keep themselves safe from HIV, primarily through safe sexual practices. New drugs have also become available in recent years. "With [these drug regimens], over three-quarters of HIV-infected patients had levels of virus in plasma suppressed to below the level at which it could be detected, and this persisted throughout follow up for as long as one year,"[12] reports UNAIDS. Long-term results are not yet available, but the early reports are promising.

The distribution of these new drugs, unfortunately, is severely restricted. UNAIDS acknowledges that the regimen "is very expensive, and the new treatments are not available to the vast majority of the world's HIV-infected people, most of whom live in developing countries."[13] Africa in particular has been devastated by AIDS (about 70 percent of the world's HIV-positive population lives on that continent), but limited resources, inadequate medical care, and poor education allow little hope of improvement. As writer Johanna McGeary says, "AIDS in Africa bears little resemblance to the American epidemic, [which is] limited to specific high-risk groups and brought under control through intensive education and expensive drug therapy. . . . [In Africa], barely a single family remains untouched . . . [and those afflicted] will all die."[14]

A young boy who is HIV-positive takes part in a World AIDS Day march in Africa, home to 70 percent of the world's HIV-positive population.

The Coming Plague?

The AIDS pandemic is the latest reminder that humankind is just as susceptible to plagues as it has always been. True, the remarkable medical advances of the last two centuries have given doctors some control over known bacteria and viruses. But the unknown is as frightening as ever. And the arrival of dangerous new diseases, say scientists, is not just a vague possibility. It is a certainty. Doctor and author Jason Eberhart-Phillips expresses the opinion of many medical experts when he says, "In retrospect, the only surprise is that HIV did not surface sooner than it did. . . . AIDS may be just the first in a series of new plagues to emerge from hiding and sweep the world during our lifetimes."[15]

Biological Warfare

Some scientists fear that terrorists may one day ignite epidemics through the use of deadly biological weapons. In his book *Outbreak Alert*, "disease detective" Jason Eberhart-Phillips, M.D., discusses the potential for such an attack and paints a lurid picture of the worst-case scenario.

The United States Office of Technology Assessment estimated that on a clear, calm night a single light plane . . . could deliver a fatal dose of anthrax spores to three million people during a short flight over Washington, D.C. . . . The plane might be seen on radar, but its deadly payload would be invisible, odorless, and tasteless. There would be no evidence that an attack had even occurred until the first cases of disease appeared in hospitals days later. By that time the bioterrorists would have vanished without a trace.

Meanwhile, panic over the fatal epidemic would quickly descend into chaos. Within days the need for tons of antibiotics would exhaust all existing stockpiles. As the death toll mounted, civil disorder in the streets might make the city ungovernable without martial law. In time, the turmoil could threaten the supremacy of the state, undermine investor confidence in world markets, and ultimately plunge the global economy into ruin. Even after the immediate effects had passed, the targeted city might remain uninhabitable for decades. . . .

A man demonstrates how easy it would be to launch deadly biological agents.

Perhaps the most disturbing aspect of such apocalyptic scenarios is how relatively simple the production of a biological weapon would be. . . . A small vial of organisms . . . could be developed into a significant arsenal in a matter of days. Only the barest knowledge of culture methods would be required, along with some fairly conventional laboratory equipment. . . . A covert bioweapons lab could be set up for a paltry $10,000. This shop of horrors would occupy a room barely twelve feet across.

The world scientific community is preparing to respond to these plagues wherever and whenever they may occur. In the United States, an organization called the Centers for Disease Control and Prevention (CDC) is at the heart of the preparedness effort. The CDC works with partners around the world to monitor known diseases—and watch for new ones. When an outbreak is detected anywhere in the world, scientists from both the CDC and local organizations can be on the spot within days or even hours to begin quarantine and containment procedures. In recent years these efforts have been instrumental in stopping several deadly outbreaks in locations including Hong Kong, the Democratic Republic of the Congo (formerly Zaire), and the southwestern United States.

Just because past outbreaks have been contained, though, does not mean that future efforts will be successful. In the opinion of microbiologist and Nobel laureate Joshua Lederberg, "Most people today are grossly overoptimistic with respect to the means we have available to forfend global epidemics comparable with the Black Death or the influenza of 1918."[16] One major factor is the increasing mobility of the human race, which means that diseases can now hop from airport to airport in a matter of hours and spread to all corners of the globe within a few days. An especially virulent disease could become established in every major city in the world before scientists even knew what hit them. In this scenario, the death toll could exceed anything humankind has ever known.

So scientists watch and wait, and hope that they will catch the next plague in time. They will probably be successful most of the time. But one slip is all it will take to let the next killer loose. Joshua Lederberg is one of many experts who believes that such a slip is inevitable. "There are catastrophes ahead," he says. "We live in evolutionary competition with . . . bacteria and viruses. There is no guarantee that we will be the survivors."[17]

Swarms

And the LORD spoke unto Moses, Go unto Pharaoh, and say unto him, Thus saith the LORD, Let my people go, that they may serve me.

And if thou refuse to let them go, behold, I will smite all thy borders with frogs: And the river shall bring forth frogs abundantly, which shall go up and come into thine house, and into thy bedchamber, and upon thy bed, and into the house of thy servants, and upon thy people, and into thine ovens, and into thy kneadingtroughs: And the frogs shall come up both on thee, and upon thy people, and upon all thy servants. . . .

And Aaron stretched out his hand over the waters of Egypt; and the frogs came up, and covered the land of Egypt.

—Exodus 8:1–4, 6

Since biblical times, recorded history has been sprinkled with accounts of swarming insects, amphibians, rodents, and other animals. Some of these creatures, such as locusts, caused incalculable damage to crops, forests, and grasslands. Others, such as the frogs of ancient Egypt, were simply unpleasant and terrifying. All swarms, however, had one thing in common: To primitive people they seemed to arrive without apparent reason, as if flung from the hand of God.

Modern scientists have a better understanding of why and how animals swarm. Understanding the phenomenon, however, fails to make it any easier to deal with. Despite the best efforts of modern science, swarms still occur, and they are still a plague on the face of the earth.

A Plague of Locusts

Of all swarming creatures, locusts are probably the most hated—and with good reason. A locust swarm can travel as much as 150 miles a day for weeks on end, chewing through field after field and leaving devastation in its wake.

A locust swarm occurs when millions, or sometimes billions, of immature locusts, called nymphs, hatch at the same time in the same area. The nymphs eat every scrap of greenery they can find, then move on in a hungry black tide. As the nymphs eat, they grow; and as they grow, they become increasingly destructive. Science writer Charles Valentine Riley describes the aftermath of an 1875 Missouri nymph swarm in this passage: "[The] portions of the country most affected were as bare as in winter. . . . An occasional oat field or low piece of prairie would remain green; but with these exceptions one might travel for days by buggy and find everything eaten off, even to the underbrush in the woods."[18]

An illustration depicts a scene from the Bible in which God sends a swarm of frogs to Egypt as a punishment. Such accounts fueled belief that plagues were an act of God.

Bugs on Trial

During the Dark Ages, the Catholic Church was heavily involved in efforts to eliminate plague insects. Prayer, excommunication, and legal action were a few of the methods tried. In his book *Millions of Monarchs, Bunches of Beetles,* entomologist Gilbert Waldbauer describes typical techniques and attitudes, as well as some specific cases.

Late in the ninth century C.E. [A.D.], the area around Rome was plagued by grasshoppers. The destruction of millions of them by the peasants did not alleviate the problem. As the story goes, Pope Steven VI prepared huge quantities of holy water and had the infested area sprinkled with it. The grasshoppers immediately disappeared.

But the church went beyond prayers, exhortations, and the sprinkling of holy water—going so far as to establish formal ecclesiastical courts that put insects on trial and condemned them if they were found guilty. . . . Insects to be prosecuted were often represented by defense counsels. The interplay between the prosecutor, who sought to condemn the insects, and the defense counsel, who fought hard to defend them, reflects the ambivalent medieval attitude toward destructive insects: Were they tormenting agents of the devil or were they punishing emissaries from God? The insects sometimes won the day and were not condemned. They were entreated to leave by prayers; the people were exhorted to pay their tithes to the church and to mend their sinful ways to relieve a punishing plague. . . .

The legal prosecution of insects continued until surprisingly recent times. . . . The most recent [recorded] prosecution occurred . . . in eastern Croatia in 1866 when the region was plagued with locusts. One of the largest of the locusts was seized and tried, found guilty, and then put to death by being thrown into water with anathemas pronounced on it and the whole species.

Destructive as it is, a nymph swarm is a mere shadow of things to come. The crawling mass of insects eventually reaches the winged adult stage and takes flight. When this happens the locusts spread out, sometimes covering an area as much as sixty miles wide. An eyewitness describes such a swarm:

The whole air . . . is filled with insects. . . . Myriads of insects blot out the sun above and cover the ground beneath and fill the air whichever way one looks. The breeze carries them swiftly past, but they come on in fresh clouds, a host of which there is no end, each of them a harmless creature which you can catch and crush in your hand, but appalling in their power of collective devastation.[19]

By the time the swarm finally dies off, it will have chewed a barren swath across the face of the earth. "Only holes in the ground showed where plants had been,"[20] lamented one swarm survivor.

If the swarm passes through cropland, the economic impact can be staggering. Between 1986 and 1989, for example, East Africa spent $275 million fighting a locust plague that nonetheless managed to destroy as much as 5 percent of the crops over huge regions. Another severe example occurred in 1874, when an enormous locust swarm in the central United States did approximately $50 million in damage. And that figure is not adjusted for

A plague of locusts swarms over an area in 1954, causing massive destruction to crops and vegetation. A locust swarm can include billions of insects and cover an area as much as sixty miles wide.

inflation. If the same swarm occurred today, economists estimate that it would cause several *billion* dollars' worth of damage.

Fighting the Plague

No such disaster, however, will ever happen—at least in the United States. Locusts have been extinct in North America since 1879, probably because their habitat was destroyed as human civilization expanded westward. In other areas of the world, though, locusts are just as much a problem today as ever. Africa still suffers the ravages of at least seven different types of locusts. South America, Australia, Russia, Asia, Arabia, and southern Europe are also affected.

Heavy insecticide use is the usual response to a locust swarm. Airplanes carrying huge drums of poison fly back and forth over the swarm, dumping chemicals as they go. The treatment does produce dead locusts—but can it stop the plague? Experts have mixed opinions. Some feel that insecticides are both effective and essential. But others, including the U.S. Office of Technology Assessment (OTA), feel differently. "While insecticides can protect standing crops, their ability to end or prevent plagues is not clear,"[21] said the OTA in a groundbreaking 1990 report. Moreover, "Massive insecticide spraying in a crisis atmosphere is costly in dollar terms; it tends to be inefficient in the short-term, ineffective in the medium-term, and misses the roots of problems in the long-term; and the potential health and environmental damage can be high."[22]

So scientists are working to discover other control methods. One recent development is a fungal spray that enters the locust's body and dissolves the creature's innards. Another experimental technique involves satellite imaging of locust-prone areas. By observing weather and vegetation data, scientists hope to predict where and when locusts will swarm.

But these techniques are unproven. And even if they do turn out to be effective, many experts feel that long-term prevention efforts are a better approach to locust control. Such efforts, however, cost money and are therefore difficult to implement in areas where money is scarce. The OTA points out, for example, that in Africa, "most . . . national and regional agencies and donor institutions are

Locusts are a type of grasshopper that are virually harmless when alone, but collectively can cause millions of dollars' worth of damage to crops.

not equipped to deal with locusts and grasshoppers on a long-term basis. . . . Development goals are sacrificed in favor of emergency management."[23] Until this situation changes, locusts will continue to do huge damage whenever and wherever they appear.

Locust Origin

At least the patterns behind "whenever and wherever they appear" are fairly well understood today. In this respect modern man has a huge advantage over his ancestors. Historically, locust swarms were frightening not just because they did so much damage, but also because they were so unpredictable. An area might suffer through locust attacks for several years in a row, then see no sign of the creatures for decades. People had no idea where the locusts came from or why they formed their destructive swarms.

Today, scientists know the answers to these questions. They have learned that locusts are just a type of grasshopper. Most of the time locusts even look and behave like proper grasshoppers.

Their bodies are a typical grasshopper color, and they keep to themselves. A locust that fits this description is said to be in the solitary phase.

If long-term weather conditions favor plant growth, however, the locust population begins to swell, rising along with the food supply. Hatching nymphs are forced into ever closer contact with each other, and when conditions become sufficiently crowded, a transformation occurs. The nymphs enter a gregarious phase in which they are strongly attracted to each other. They congregate in dense clumps and begin to exhibit swarm behavior. Their bodies even change as they grow: A gregarious locust is larger and more brightly colored than its solitary cousin.

The gregarious nymphs will stick together until they become winged adults. Then they will take off together and travel as a swarm throughout their lifetimes. If humans are lucky, the swarm will starve in a barren desert or fall into the sea. But as entomologist Gilbert Waldbauer writes, "If they land in a favorable place with abundant vegetation, they will lay eggs—countless millions of them that may give rise to another devastating population of locusts."[24] The cycle continues until weather conditions or other circumstances reduce the locust population enough for the insects to revert to their solitary phase.

Cause and Effect

Uncommon weather is the culprit behind many insect outbreaks. Such is the case with the African army worm, which is the larval stage of the night flying moth. Army worm outbreaks usually occur when the onset of the rainy season follows a drought. These conditions trigger an egg-laying frenzy among adult female moths. Within two months, millions of tiny worms emerge from the eggs and go on the march. They travel in squirming masses from one field to the next, eating as they go. "They will attack almost any kind of grass, including sugarcane and maize," explains agricultural expert R. A. Bell. "The latter will be stripped until there is nothing left but midribs and stalks."[25] In recent years army worm outbreaks have been a contributing factor to famine conditions throughout Africa.

Other swarms are the result of human habitation. India, for example, is overrun by rats—a plague directly related to the country's spreading human population. "In recent decades, growing numbers of people moving through the area have drastically altered the habitat, hacking down the forests and decimating the wildlife. Today, what isn't irrigated farmland is largely desert, with islands of scrub overrun by mesquite and other weeds. Such conditions are ideal for rats,"[26] explains author Zai Whitaker. How bad is the problem? According to Whitaker, Indian rats steal enough grain each year to feed the country's human population for months.

Poison in the Seas

Some swarms result from a combination of climatic and human impacts. This is the case with harmful algal blooms (HABs). HABs occur after microscopic ocean-dwelling algae have multiplied out of control due to favorable weather and nutrient conditions. Favorable nutrient conditions can occur naturally, but there

African army worms eat through a maize plant. Recent army worm outbreaks have contributed to famine conditions in Africa.

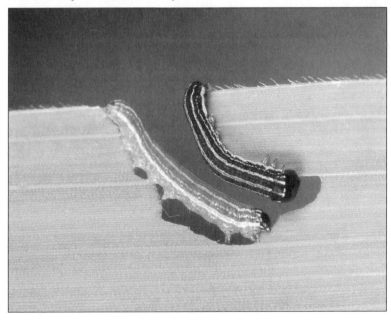

A Plague of Rats

In the year 1284, the town of Hameln, Germany, was allegedly overrun by a plague of rats. Hameln's story—with a few embellishments—is told in the popular tale *The Pied Piper of Hamelin*. In his famous children's book of the same name, poet Robert Browning describes the town's situation.

> Rats!
> They fought the dogs and killed the cats,
> And bit the babies in the cradles,
> And ate the cheese out of the vats,
> And licked the soup from the cooks' own ladles,
> Split open the kegs of salted sprats,
> Made nests inside men's Sunday hats,
> And even spoiled the women's chats,
> By drowning their speaking
> With shrieking and squeaking
> In fifty different sharps and flats.

And in "The Ratcatcher," another version of the story, author Charles Marelles writes the following.

> A very long time ago the town of Hamel in Germany was invaded by bands of rats, the like of which had never been seen before nor will ever be again.
>
> They were great black creatures that ran boldly in broad daylight through the streets, and swarmed so, all over the houses, that people at last could not put their hand or foot down anywhere without touching one. When dressing in the morning they found them in their breeches and petticoats, in their pockets and in their boots; and when they wanted a morsel to eat, the voracious horde had swept away everything from cellar to garret. The night was even worse. As soon as the lights were out, these untiring nibblers set to work. And everywhere, in the ceilings, in the floors, in the cupboards, at the doors, there was a chase and a rummage, and so furious a noise of gimlets, pincers, and saws, that a deaf man could not have rested for one hour together.

is growing evidence that human agricultural runoff is changing the composition of coastal waters and creating conditions that encourage HABs.

During an HAB, millions upon millions of algae spread out over huge areas of the ocean, clouding the water and entering the bodies of fish and shellfish. These infected creatures may eventually be caught and eaten by humans—and the results can be deadly. In 1799, for example, more than one hundred people in what is now Alaska died after eating toxin-contaminated shellfish.

Such a death toll would be unusual today, when improved medical care means fewer deaths. But HAB-related sicknesses are not to be taken lightly. They occur regularly, and they can still kill. As recently as 1987, more than a hundred people on Canada's Prince Edward Island became ill and three lost their lives after eating poisoned mussels. And in addition to the occasional fatal case, thousands of nonlethal HAB poisonings are treated each year. The average annual HAB-related health care cost in the United States alone is estimated at $22 million, but the true total is probably much higher; medical experts believe that most HAB-caused illnesses go unreported.

HABs may also affect people indirectly by killing commercially important fish long before they get the chance to land on a human plate. These "fish kills," as they are called, may be immense. In 1997, for example, an HAB-related fish kill that washed up along the Texas shoreline contained an estimated 21 million carcasses. A fish kill of this magnitude is an economic disaster for fisheries. It also deals a crippling blow to a region's tourism industry as travelers avoid the infested area.

Between their effects on fisheries, tourism, and other industries, HABs are expensive. It is estimated that the average annual cost of HABs to U.S. commercial interests is about $25 million—and that figure can occasionally be much higher. In 1997, for instance, the Maryland seafood and recreational fishing industries suffered a $50 million loss in just a few months as the result of an HAB. And in 1976 an HAB off the New Jersey shoreline caused an estimated $1 billion in losses to shellfish-related businesses.

Bare Trees

The spruce budworm of North America is another swarming pest that can have a significant monetary impact. In its larval phase the spruce budworm feeds on the needles and needle buds of fir trees. If enough budworms infest a tree they may eat every scrap of foliage, eventually killing the tree. The budworm pinch is therefore felt mostly by paper manufacturers, lumber merchants, and other businesses that depend on wood.

Spruce budworms are always present in their home range, which extends throughout the forests of North America. Every forty years or so, however, these creatures undergo a population explosion, increasing from a norm of about 26 million worms per square mile to as many as 26 billion in that same area—a thousandfold increase. And the explosion may spread over thousands of square miles, with devastating effects. "I remember stopping my car to look at a badly infected patch of fir," says writer Bret

A spruce budworm feeds on the needles of a fir tree. Outbreaks of these insects can cause severe hardship for the loggers and other businesses that depend on the wood.

Wallach, who witnessed one particularly severe outbreak. "[The worms] were eating the needles around them, then spinning a bit of white filament and dropping down to the next branch. Bare of needles but wrapped in coils of filament, the firs were like dried-up Christmas trees tossed out in January with angel hair still on them."[27]

One of the worst spruce budworm outbreaks in recent history plagued the state of Maine from the late 1970s until about 1985. Trees representing more than 26 million cords of wood (about 3.3 billion cubic feet) died during the infestation. Fearing for their livelihoods, panicky loggers cut down huge tracts of damaged trees before they could rot and become economically useless. By the time the budworm outbreak had run its course, nearly two thousand square miles of woodland had been cleared, forever changing the character of Maine's forests.

The Cicada Cycle

Compared to spruce budworms, locusts, army worms, HABs, and most other swarming animals, periodical cicadas are marvels of predictability. These grasshopper-like creatures, which occur in every U.S. region east of the Great Plains, appear on schedule every thirteen or seventeen years. After emerging, they swarm for several weeks—just long enough to eat a little tree sap, mate, and then deposit a few hundred eggs in slit tree branches. They die soon after their reproductive duties are done.

Like locusts, periodical cicadas start their lives as wingless nymphs that emerge millions at a time from the ground. Most of these nymphs reach the adult stage within a few days of each other, causing a sudden explosion of bugs in the emergence area. The resulting cicada population can be mind-bogglingly immense: One brood that emerged near Chicago in 1956, for example, was estimated to include almost a billion insects.

Despite their large numbers, cicadas do little damage to their environment. "[They] do not kill trees in their feeding, and at no point in their lives do they hurt garden vegetables or flowering plants," explains writer Sue Hubbell. In fact, she adds, "They are bugs of such innocence and beauty and specialness that their appearance,

Cicada Feast

A cicada swarm disappears naturally after a few weeks. But for those who cannot wait, experts propose a bold solution: Eat the crawling critters.

In the *Time* magazine article "First Crunch, Then Munch," University of Chicago ecology professor Monte Lloyd describes how cicadas taste. "They are quite good, like avocado and new potato mixed." The article suggests a sample recipe: Dip cicadas in batter and fry until golden brown. Serve with cocktail sauce or sour cream, or use as a pizza topping.

Mike Wyatt, another bold bug eater, offers this advice in the *Backpacker* magazine article "How to Eat Bugs": "Newly hatched cicadas are best because their shells haven't hardened. With adults, pluck wings and legs before cooking. Place cicadas in pan and roast over heat for 10–15 minutes; when dry, grind coarsely and sprinkle on food for a nutty taste. Or drop cicadas in boiling water, coat with red pepper, garlic, and ground bay leaf. Or stir-fry with garlic, then add your freeze-dried meal packet."

And in answer to the question—"Is it safe for my pets to eat cicadas?"—the Cicada Mania website offers the following: "Yes, but they may choke on them or gorge themselves and become ill. Keep an eye on your pets to make sure they don't eat too many. Big stupid dogs love them."

As a novel solution to a cicada swarm, some people have taken to eating the reportedly tasty insects.

Like a locust swarm, mayfly swarms can be an awesome and frightening sight, covering the sky with millions of insects. Unlike locusts, mayflies do not destroy crops.

one would think, would be regarded with interest and appreciation."[28] But this is not the case. Most people dislike cicadas and some are terrified of them. Some people poison, smash, and squash as many bugs as possible in a frantic attempt to keep the "monsters" at bay. For such people, the negative psychological aspects of the cicada plague are much more harmful than any physical damage the insects may inflict.

Mountains of Mayflies

People living along the western edge of Lake Erie are all too familiar with the psychological stress a cyclical plague can cause. For a few predictable days each year the area is overrun by an insect plague of its own when millions of mayfly nymphs emerge from lakes and rivers, then metamorphose into inch-long, winged adults. Like cicadas, mayflies do little harm. But their sheer numbers are enough to frighten almost anyone.

On June 25, 1996, the city of Port Clinton, Ohio, experienced the largest mayfly swarm in recent memory. Then mayor Thomas Brown describes the arrival of the winged invaders: "A dark cloud appeared over the stadium. This cloud turned out to be a swarm of mayflies that descended on the crowd. Many people in the audience were screaming and swatting, others were laughing as everything in sight became coated with mayflies. . . . I was covered from head to toe."[29]

The mayflies gathered around any light source, including streetlights, shop windows, and vending machines. There they bashed themselves to death and fell by the thousands to the streets and sidewalks below. Cars and motorcycles skidded on the gooey carcasses, leading the city to post warning signs along highways. Shopkeepers swept their sidewalks constantly to keep their doorsteps free of bug bodies. And walkers had to endure a gruesome crunching sound with each step. "It's like running over Rice Krispies," shuddered one resident. "You can hear them popping."[30] Snowplows were brought out to cart away the corpses. By the time the swarm had run its course the city had scraped thirty-five truckloads of mayflies off its streets.

Mayfly swarms of this magnitude are not seen every year. However, conditions seem ripe for an increase in mayfly activity. Decreasing pollution in area lakes and rivers is increasing the nymph population, which will undoubtedly give rise to larger adult swarms. The bugs themselves will continue to be mostly harmless: "They carry no diseases; they don't bite; they are not blood feeding; they feed on no crops or organisms,"[31] explains biologist Steven Burian. But it is certain that the mayflies will continue to inspire fear and loathing among the human population. Why? As Burian says, "Some people just don't like being covered with live insects."[32]

Plague Control

Because the mayfly life cycle is so short, extermination efforts are not practical. Instead, residents of mayfly-prone areas have learned to live with the annual invasion. An article in the Ohio Lake Erie Commission's bimonthly newsletter explains how:

Educational programs and signage were developed to inform residents about the "dos and dont's" of dealing with mayflies. City-wide blackouts are encouraged during peak hatch times to keep mayflies from swarming toward light sources . . . [and a grant] even helped fund special electrical switches that allow city safety service crews to easily turn off street lights to keep the mayflies at bay.[33]

This "live-and-let-live" attitude is a feasible response to swarms of harmless creatures like mayflies and cicadas. But when human lives and livelihoods are at stake, the balance changes. No farmer is content to sit back and watch locusts or army worms destroy acres of cropland, and no government can afford to sit idly by while its citizens die from seafood poisoning. Harmful plagues call for action. In the case of insect infestations, that action usually involves heavy insecticide application. Rodent plagues call for mass extermination efforts, including trapping and poisoning. And HABs are controlled by careful monitoring of ocean waters and tight regulation of the affected industries and areas.

These types of crisis management, unfortunately, are limited in their effectiveness. By the time they are used, the plague—whatever it may be—is already raging out of control. Human efforts may reduce the plague's impact, but they are unlikely to stop the scourge altogether.

Disaster . . . or Correction?

There is a good reason for this. Swarms are, after all, simply nature's way of correcting an imbalance. Too much greenery in the desert? Send in a plague of locusts to get rid of the plants. Extra nutrients in the water? Grow millions of algae to gobble it up. "Plagues only manifest as a 'natural phenomenon' to try and correct what we have done to nature or to find a new balance after changes in weather patterns or some other natural disaster,"[34] points out one author. Until the earth regains its normal state, the swarm will continue—and nature will resist human attempts to interfere with the correction process.

Many experts feel that emergency responses to swarms are therefore doomed to failure. Long-term prevention and control programs, they say, would be a better way of managing animal explosions. But it is hard to get people to adopt this approach. Prevention efforts are expensive, which makes them easy to postpone when no immediate danger threatens. The fact that prevention procedures yield no visible results is also a problem. As the OTA notes in reference to the African locust problem, "Starting down a different route now is likely to have long-term benefits [but] the results of taking a new direction are likely to be less visible, less dramatic, and perhaps less satisfying for donors in the short term than spraying millions of hectares with insecticides."[35]

India has begun extermination efforts to control the rat plague that afflicts their country. Here, Indian villagers tally the number of rats caught in a day's work.

Even if prevention programs *were* implemented around the world, success would be far from certain. Natural imbalances must be corrected, and people cannot halt the process forever. Many scientists even feel that in some cases, it is not worth trying. Let nature have her way, they say, and the plague will eventually disappear on its own. In this view, it is time to accept swarms as an unchangeable fact of life on earth.

Bioinvasion

Every country in the world is under constant attack. The attackers are not human armies; rather, they are foreign insects, animals, and plants that are being carried, blown, or otherwise transported across borders into new areas.

Most introduced species either die out or fail to have a lasting effect on a new region. Some, however, become major pests, creating economic and ecological effects severe enough to destroy industries and ecosystems. An attack of this magnitude is known as a biological invasion, or bioinvasion for short—and a bioinvasion that affects human structures or endeavors may cause enough damage to qualify as a devastating plague indeed.

The Bioinvasion Process and Outlook

The seeds of a bioinvasion are sown when a plant or animal moves, either by accident or by design, into a new region of the world. The foreign plant or animal is called an exotic; natural residents of the region are called natives.

The great majority of exotics die out quickly. Some, however, find that they can survive in the new area—and a small percentage of the survivors discover that conditions are absolutely perfect. Food is abundant, the climate is favorable, and their natural predators and illnesses are absent. In short, their ecological niche is empty, and they immediately go about filling it. The exotics start to multiply quickly, often crowding out native species in the process and sometimes causing significant economic and environmental damage. When this stage is reached, the exotic species has earned the title of biological invader.

At its heart, bioinvasion is a natural process. "Some degree of movement through the Earth's barriers has always been a part of life, of course—no natural community is hermetically sealed," explains writer and researcher Chris Bright. "A shift in the prevailing sea breeze might bring a colony of bats to an island; an increase in rainfall might allow forest out onto a prairie."[36] But the process has accelerated greatly in recent history. In Hawaii, for example, "an average of eighteen new insects or other arthropods have established themselves every year over the past half century or so. That's more than a MILLION times the natural rate of invasion for that group of organisms,"[37] according to Bright.

How big is the problem? Currently, harmful exotic species in the United States alone have a measurable economic impact of over $123 billion each year. And as the U.S. Office of Technology

Entomologists examine a Mexican weevil, an imported pest that has been killing rare bromeliad plants in Florida. Biological invaders like this Mexican weevil have a huge economic and ecological impact on the United States.

The Tens Rule

An organism that finds its way to distant shores does not automatically invade the new territory. In fact, quite the opposite is true, explains research scientist Chris Bright in his book *Life out of Bounds: Bioinvasion in a Borderless World.*

Most [exotics] do not succeed in establishing themselves in their new ranges—they just die out. Even those that do establish themselves will not necessarily have a detectable ecological effect. . . .

The proportion of exotics that cause serious trouble is difficult to estimate, but a very rough rule of thumb, sometimes called the "tens rule," is that 10 percent of exotics introduced into an area will succeed in establishing breeding populations, and 10 percent of those will go on to launch a major invasion. When that happens, [the exotic] has escaped the predators, diseases, and other factors that kept it in check in its native range, and has found nothing comparable in its new range. It is facing organisms that did not evolve in its presence and that may not be adapted to competing with it or escaping from it. . . . The result is usually lots of exotic and a lot less of everything else.

Since the global economy is continually showering exotics over the earth's surface, there is little consolation in the fact that 90 percent of these impacts are "duds" and only 1 percent of them really detonate. The bombardment is continual, and so are the detonations.

Assessment points out, "The figures represent only a part of the total documented and possible costs—that is, they do not include a large number of species known to be costly but for which little or no economic data [are] available."[38] The full cost of the U.S. bioinvasion situation may never be known, but it is certainly immense. Expand the impact to global proportions and it becomes evident that biological invaders are a plague indeed.

The Human Factor

The bioinvasion acceleration is due to humankind's global mobility, which is a relatively recent phenomenon. In ages past, natural barriers such as oceans, deserts, and mountain ranges ensured that most organisms stayed in their home areas. But those barriers began to come down in the early 1500s, when global exploration became possible and popular. Travelers to distant lands unknowingly transported rats and snakes that had stowed away in their ships and wagons, as well as insects, seeds, and spores hidden in their hair and on their clothing. And they purposely carried livestock, plants, and other exotics that they hoped to introduce when they reached their destinations.

Sailing ships full of colonists arrive at Jamestown. Global exploration and colonization paved the way for bioinvasion as the travelers both knowingly and unknowingly introduced countless exotics to new lands.

Most of these introductions proved harmless and many were actually beneficial, at least to humans. Essential crops and animals were established around the world as human colonies expanded to new areas. These exotics fed the colonists, enabling them to survive and thrive in unfamiliar lands.

The exotics introduced during the first wave of expansion were pretty basic: corn, wheat, pigs, chickens. Once a colony was established, however, there usually occurred a secondary wave of exotic introduction during which nonessential, but pleasant and familiar, species were imported. This process, called acclimatization, was designed to make the colony feel more like home. Chris Bright describes the attitude of Australian colonists during the mid-1800s: "Australian nature appeared to be badly flawed and the fortunes of the colony depended on its correction. . . . Aborigines might content themselves with roast monitor lizard, but the landscape would have to be stocked according to the colonists' tastes, with rabbit, deer, and pheasant."[39]

Billions of Rabbits

The colonists' taste for rabbit, however, would eventually spark one of the costliest biological invasions in human history. In the middle to late 1800s, a plague of rabbits exploded in Australia with a violence from which the continent has never fully recovered.

The plague started innocently enough in 1859, when an Australian acclimatization society imported and released twenty-four wild rabbits in south Australia. Rabbit hunting was popular at the time, and it was hoped that the rabbits would reproduce and form colonies big enough to sustain this sport.

They did—and then some. By 1875, a mere sixteen years after the initial twenty-four rabbits were released, the wild population was spreading so quickly that it came to be called the "grey blanket." Farmers watched helplessly as the creatures devastated crops and honeycombed valuable fields with burrows and tunnels. A Rabbit Destruction Act was passed in an effort to control the animals, but they were too well established. Nothing seemed to work. In desperation, many farmers erected miles-long fences to stop the

The release of twenty-four rabbits in south Australia in 1859 eventually led to a huge plague of rabbits that would become one of the costliest biological invasions in history.

invaders, but this tactic failed partly because, "In plague proportions, there were so many rabbits piled up by the fences that [they] acted as a ladder for others that simply walked over the fence."[40] By 1881, rabbits had destroyed so much cropland that farmers began to abandon their fields.

The economic consequences of the plague were staggering. One writer explains the impact on grazing and farmland: "In good seasons there may have been one billion rabbits. As 16 rabbits eat as much as one sheep, this is equivalent to approximately 60 million sheep and the consequent loss of production."[41] Eventually some control was obtained by releasing a virus deadly to rabbits but not to other species. The rabbit problem was greatly reduced, but it proved impossible to eliminate. In fact, Australian farmers are plagued by rabbits to this day. "The economic impact of present-day rabbit populations is not well quantified, but is estimated to be on the order of $90 million [per year] in lost production and about $20 million spent on control."[42]

And all because a group of well-meaning European settlers decided to import two dozen rabbits.

The American Acclimatization Society

Some of the exotic species that plague humans today were deliberately introduced hundreds of years ago by "acclimatization societies"—organizations created solely to spread exotics around the world. The American Acclimatization Society, founded in the late 1800s, was one such society. Its goal was "the introduction and acclimatization of such foreign varieties of the animal and vegetable kingdoms as may be useful or interesting."

The American Acclimatization Society found birds especially interesting. In his article "The Birds," author Joe Miller describes the origin and lasting results of this interest.

In 1890, a group of aristocrats gathered in New York's Central Park, carrying sixty delicate, small-beaked birds brought from Europe.

This pedantic consortium was bound by a common goal of populating North America with every bird mentioned in Shakespearean verse. The thrushes, chaffinches, nightingales, and skylarks they'd imported had all died out. But with European starlings they hit pay dirt. The little birds took flight from downtown Manhattan and made nests and multiplied. Now European starlings are among the most common birds in the United States—and Americans must suffer the legacy of an otherwise forgettable line from *Henry IV*: "Nay, I'll have a starling shall be taught to speak nothing but 'Mortimer.'. . ."

A natural history biologist for the [Missouri Department of Conservation] says [that] these innocent-looking creatures are nothing short of aviary gangsters. True criminals, they muscle into the turf of native birds and rob them of food and shelter. "They are the thugs of the bird world," he once wrote. . . . "Among those who know and love birds, the starling is almost universally hated. They are seen as noisy, dirty, greedy, and mean."

They are also everywhere. Today, there are an estimated 200 million starlings in North America—all thanks to the efforts of the American Acclimatization Society.

The Ballast Problem

Australia's rabbits were intentionally introduced to the continent. But many of the world's most damaging biological invasions have been accidents that occurred as the result of human travel. Such accidents are called biotic spills, and when they happen, they can change the very face of the land and seas.

The shipping industry is especially guilty of causing biotic spills. The reason lies in ships' ballast tanks, which are huge holding containers into which water can be pumped to stabilize a vessel. A ship sucks in ballast water as needed from the ocean around it. That water, of course, is full of fish, crabs, plankton, and other creatures. Depending on the ship's itinerary, those creatures may be carried hundreds or even thousands of miles before being flushed back into the sea. Many of the exotics will die in the process. But some will survive, and some of the survivors will explode into full-blown plagues.

Leidy's comb jelly, a jellyfish smaller than the human thumb, is one recent example. Around 1982 a ship carried some of these creatures from their home range off the east coast of the Americas into the Black Sea, where they were released in a routine ballast water purge. The jellies immediately launched one of the worst marine invasions ever recorded. By 1988 the sea was nearly solid with the creatures—"but the anchovies and other fish that account for the sea's traditional catch had largely disappeared. The jelly apparently provoked the collapse of the Black Sea ecosystem,"[43] writes Chris Bright. The collapse was a disaster for the industries that depended on that ecosystem.

A less spectacular but even more damaging creature is the zebra mussel, which traveled via ballast tank from its native Russia to North America around 1988. These inch-long creatures cement themselves by the hundreds of thousands to hard underwater surfaces such as

Zebra mussels embed themselves in docks, pipelines, and boat hulls, causing millions of dollars of damage annually.

pipelines, docks, and boat hulls. They are notorious for clogging the intakes of city water systems, power plant cooling systems, and boat engines. The cost of clearing these intakes currently runs about $200 million per year in the United States, with a cumulative total expected to reach $5 billion by the year 2002.

Eating the Cities

While marine creatures hide in a ship's ballast tanks, insect invaders lurk in the cargo hold above. Shipments of wood, plants, and other biological materials are especially likely to harbor exotic insects. And when these shipments reach their destinations, they may unleash new plagues upon the land.

The Formosan termite is one such plague. Concealed inside wooden planks, these creatures arrived in New Orleans on military cargo ships in the 1940s. The termites established colonies in New Orleans' historic French Quarter and started eating. By the turn of the century the insects had infested 80 percent of the city's historic structures and almost all of its private residences, causing widespread structural damage. "You can't have people over," complained an infestation victim. "You don't want them to step in the wrong spot and go through the floor."[44]

Formosans are much more destructive than North America's native termites, mostly because their colonies are so large. "[They are] capable of building colonies of up to 10 million writhing white bugs, which devour an average of 1,000 pounds of wood a year. Native termite colonies, one-tenth the size, eat a meager 7 pounds per year,"[45] explains one journalist. The Formosans' appetite causes an estimated $300 million in damage each year in New Orleans alone.

To make matters worse, these invaders are spreading across the country. Today, Formosan termites infest eleven states including Georgia, North and South Carolina, and California, causing nationwide damage totaling about $1 billion per year. Pest control experts are trying to stop the problem, but Formosans are proving incredibly tough to kill. It is possible that they may one day be controlled to some degree, but it is unlikely that they will be wiped out. As one entomologist says, "Eradicating them is just not going to happen."[46]

Since coming ashore on a ship in Alabama in the 1930s, red fire ants from Brazil have wreaked havoc in the United States with their destructive habits.

Plague Underground

The red fire ant, a native of Brazil, is another billion-dollar-plus invader of the United States that is here to stay. Sometime in the 1930s a ship infested with these pests docked in Mobile, Alabama. The fire ants escaped the ship and established colonies on land, then began to multiply outward at a rate of about thirty miles per year. Today, the ants' range spreads from Florida to the Carolinas, from Tennessee to Texas, and their territory is still expanding northward and westward.

Fire ants have some unusually destructive habits. They are attracted to electrical current and often chew through wires and cables. In North Carolina, says one writer, the ants "have been damaging airport runway lights, burning out electric outlets, and short-circuiting traffic lights as dozens of the insects cram into the control boxes and eat through insulation."[47] The ants may also tunnel beneath roadways, weakening the ground and causing the pavement to collapse. They have been known to devour crop seeds during times of drought, sometimes ruining entire plantings. And even the ants' homes are costly: The rock-hard, foot-high mounds that mark fire ant colonies do hundreds of millions of dollars' worth of damage to U.S. farm equipment each year.

Fire ants are poisonous, too. They attack as a group and use their venom to kill newborn domestic livestock, pets, wildlife, and sometimes even people. Although human deaths from fire ant bites are rare (only about fifty fatalities have ever been confirmed), many people become ill from the insects' poison. An estimated seventy thousand people receive medical treatment for fire ant bites each year.

Harmful Plants

Although animals get most of the attention when it comes to bioinvasion, they are only part of the problem. Exotic plants, too, can become invaders, and their economic effects may rival those of the worst animal pests.

The melaleuca, a tree native to Australia, is a good example of such an invader. Melaleuca trees were introduced to Florida in the early 1900s as part of an effort to tame the swampy Everglades. (Because they consume vast quantities of water, melaleuca have a stabilizing effect on wet ground.) The trees grew well in their new home and soon spread throughout south Florida. Developers rejoiced over the success of their experiment.

The developers had overlooked one important fact, however. Due to their tinder-dry bark and oil-filled leaves, melaleuca are explosively flammable. And because melaleuca fires are oil-based, they are incredibly difficult to extinguish. In the decades since melaleuca took hold in south Florida, the trees have been responsible for several major blazes, including one in Fort Lauderdale in May 1985 that caused more than $1 billion in damage.

The blue gum eucalyptus tree, another plague bioinvader, has caused

The blue gum eucalyptus is one of the most flammable tree species on earth. It has been a factor in several major California fires.

similar problems in California. The eucalyptus may be even more flammable than the melaleuca: "No other species on earth contains as much volatile combustibility in a given area of land surface,"[48] says a fire protection official. Eucalyptuses have contributed to several major California blazes, most notably the Oakland–Berkeley Hills fire of 1991. According to one source, the fire "killed 25 people, injured 150 others, destroyed 2,449 single-family dwellings and 437 apartment and condominium units, burned over 1,600 acres, and did an estimated $1.5 billion in damage."[49]

Eradication Efforts

Considering the dollar amounts involved, it is no surprise that officials are eager to stamp out harmful exotics. But the eradication of biological invaders is easier said than done. By their nature, bioinvaders are hardy species that multiply quickly, and humans often find it impossible to keep up. In south Florida, for example, a melaleuca control project is currently removing one acre of the pesky plants each day, but the trees' range is expanding at fifty times that rate. Massive application of herbicides might speed things up, but officials are reluctant to adopt such aggressive measures because of the potential for damage to other species.

Other invaders are simply too tough to kill. The U.S. government learned this lesson the hard way between 1957 and 1977, when red fire ants became the target of a $200-million insecticide campaign that dusted millions of acres with poisonous chemicals. Most native insects died in the bombardment—but the fire ants survived, then expanded into the natives' now-empty territory. Rather than wiping out the invaders, the eradication program probably encouraged their spread by killing most of the ants' competitors. This disastrous campaign, called by one scientist the "Vietnam of entomology,"[50] taught officials to think carefully before taking action against biological invaders.

Though harmful exotics are difficult to eradicate, they can often be controlled to some degree. Poison bait, for example, is being tested in New Orleans against the city's Formosan termites, with promising early results. Florida's Dade County has banned residents from planting new melaleuca trees, thus stopping the spread of the fire-starter into populous areas. And the damage potential of zebra mussels is being reduced in hard-hit areas by the installation of special screens that prevent the creatures from infesting water intakes.

Prevention

All of these efforts, no matter how successful, fall under the category of damage control. A better response to exotics is to prevent them from spreading in the first place. As one scientist notes, "The first line of defense against invasive exotics is not to allow them into the country. . . . It is far more difficult to deal with introduced species once they are established than it is to keep them out."[51]

To this end, many countries have established strict import control policies. In the United States, for example, the Department of Agriculture's Animal and Plant Health Inspection Service (APHIS) employs thousands of plant protection and quarantine inspectors at airports, seaports, and border stations around the country. APHIS employees use a variety of methods, including X-rays, trained dogs, and visual inspection, to detect and prevent the entry of undesirable exotics.

An Australian Quarantine and Inspection Service dog sniffs luggage at Sydney International Airport in an effort to control bioinvasion problems.

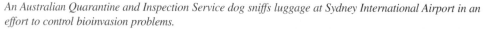

New Zealand, an island nation with significant bioinvasion problems, has implemented some especially tough import restrictions. In 1996 the country's government enacted legislation called the Hazardous Substances and New Organisms Act (HSNOA) that prohibits the import of any new exotic organism until its potential impact has been evaluated. It is too early to know whether HSNOA will meet its goals, but concerned scientists around the world nonetheless welcome the act as an important precedent in the field of biological invasion.

Limited Effectiveness

But New Zealand is just one country among many, and legislation like HSNOA is not the worldwide norm. Most nations remain reluctant to adopt tough standards. Even in the United States, one of the stricter countries in terms of border inspection, "Federal and most state agencies have adopted a policy of assuming that a species will pose no problems unless proven otherwise and, therefore, have not demanded that individuals wishing to import a plant or animal species demonstrate that its introduction will prove innocuous," comments writer Daniel Simberloff. And further, he continues, "Funding for the enforcement of the meager regulations that now govern the movement of exotics is woefully inadequate. . . . Current federal laws are only invoked after a species is already in the U.S.—in other words, too late."[52]

Even in situations where regulations are in effect and enforced, the movement of exotics can be difficult to detect. Snakes, for example, sometimes crawl into the wheel wells of airplanes, only to be whisked halfway around the world and deposited, unnoticed, in a new land. Exotic seeds may be carried hundreds or thousands of miles in travelers' clothing, hair, and baggage. And a single potted plant can harbor a colony of fire ants. To the casual observer, successfully preventing exotic invasions seems impossible—and the experts agree. "I doubt we'll be able to keep the thing out in the long haul," says a biologist for the Pest Exclusion Branch of the California Department of Food and Agriculture in reference to the red fire ant. "The best we can hope for is a delaying factor."[53]

But the biggest threat may be the one that is unknown. Many industries, including agriculture, horticulture, and fisheries, depend on the import of exotics for their survival, and these imports tend to be made with little or no consideration of the potentially harmful consequences. Although most of the animals and plants introduced by these industries will probably have positive effects, it is inevitable that a small percentage will eventually become serious pests.

What the Future Holds

There is some good news on the biological invasion front. Governments and scientists around the world are becoming aware of the problem. They are discussing solutions and taking action.

The 1992 Convention on Biological Diversity was the first step toward worldwide regulation of invasive species. Delegates from 168 countries signed the convention, which addressed mostly the ecological rather than the economic effects of bioinvasion. Although the agreement contained some controversial points that are still under discussion, experts agree that "the results . . . could well be the start of a global system for controlling non-native species."[54]

Some countries are also following New Zealand's lead and taking action at the national level. The United States, for instance, established a National Invasive Species Council (NISC) in 1999. The council's mission is to ensure that federal agency activities concerning invasive species are coordinated, complementary, cost-efficient, and effective. The details of the operation have not yet been worked out, but the mere existence of the NISC is proof that the biological invasion problem is being taken seriously—a big change for a government that until recently was, as one scientist says, "much more concerned with bringing new foreign species *into* the United States."[55]

But regulations can only go so far. The base truth is that old habits are hard to break—and as far as humankind is concerned, the import of exotic species is a very old habit indeed. It has also been mostly a successful one. As one science writer points out, "Ninety-nine percent of crop plants in the United States are non-native, as are all our livestock except the turkey. . . . We have reaped enormous benefits from non-native species."[56] Past triumphs will encourage the deliberate introduction of new species to continue. The accidental spread of exotics will also increase along with human mobility. And no matter how elaborate the prevention efforts, new invasions *will* erupt. When, where, and how bad? The very nature of plagues makes those questions impossible to answer.

Blights

Humankind's evolutionary ancestors were walking the earth for millions of years before modern man came along. These ancestors were hunter/gatherers, surviving on animal kills and whatever edible plants they could find.

About ten thousand years ago, however, that lifestyle changed when humans learned how to prepare and eat grains, legumes, and other plant products. People quickly realized that these new foods were not only tasty, they were also much more convenient than the traditional diet. Soon humans were deliberately planting fields full of wheat, rice, beans, and other food crops to supplement their hunting activities, and before long, organized agriculture had become a way of life. The hunter/gatherer days were mostly forgotten, and humankind became dependent on crops for its survival.

For the most part this dependence has worked out well. But it has also created one big problem. Crops, like humans, can get sick and die from viral, bacterial, and fungal diseases (blights). And when they do, the people who count on those crops may suffer economic ruin, famine, and perhaps even starvation. In its worst form, a crop blight can explode into a plague severe enough to bring death to millions of people.

The Rise of the Potato

The roots of history's worst famine were planted in the 1500s and 1600s, when Spanish explorers discovered potatoes in South America. The Spaniards brought this food home with them to Europe, where it quickly became a dietary staple.

A huge number of potatoes can be grown in a tiny plot of land. This made the vegetable especially popular in poor countries, including impoverished Ireland, which in the sixteenth century was populated mostly by tenant farmers and landless laborers (agricultural workers whose position in society was much like the one occupied by today's migrant pickers). Plant pathologist George W. Hudler explains the potato's appeal: "Oppressed Irish peasants, trying to eke out livings on small plots of land for which they paid exorbitant rents, were especially receptive to the new food. In fact, they were so receptive that by the late eighteenth century, a typical tenant family of husband, wife, and four children consumed about 250 pounds of potatoes each week!"[57]

Irish women dig up a crop of potatoes. The typical Irish tenent family in the late eighteenth century was dependent on the potato crop and consumed about 250 pounds of potatoes each week.

For the first time in hundreds of years, the Irish were getting enough food on a regular basis, and the result was a general upswing in national health. Fewer people became ill, more children were born, and fewer babies died in infancy. Thanks primarily to the potato, says Hudler, "From 1800 to 1845, the population of Ireland nearly doubled—from 4.5 to 8 million people."[58]

Disaster Strikes

But in the summer of 1845, disaster struck. "A fatal malady has broken out amongst the potato crop," wrote Dr. John Lindley, editor of a local agricultural gazette, on August 23, 1845. He continued:

> The disease consists in a gradual decay of the leaves and stem, which become a putrid mass, and the tubers are affected by degrees in a similar way. The first obvious sign is the appearance on the edge of the leaf of a black spot which gradually spreads; the gangrene then attacks the [stems], and in a few days the latter are decayed, emitting a peculiar and rather offensive odour. When the attack is severe, the tubers also decay. . . . As to cure for this distemper, there is none.[59]

Farmers all over Ireland watched helplessly as the mysterious disease turned their fields to mush, destroying the food they were counting on to get them through the coming winter. Some people managed to dig up their crops before the illness struck, but that did no good; the blight just attacked the harvested potatoes, turning them to slime on the shelves. Nothing seemed to stop the disease, and by the time autumn ended, the blight had claimed about a third of the country's potato crop.

Although the destruction of the potatoes made for a hungry winter, most people got through the cold months without too much trouble. A little thinner and a little weaker, the Irish peasants planted their fields again in the spring of 1846, counting on a good potato harvest to make up for the previous year's disaster. But it was not to be. The blight struck again in the summer of 1846, destroying even more potatoes than it had the first time around.

And then the winter arrived.

Starving peasants clamor at the gates of a workhouse during the Irish potato famine. In ten years, Ireland lost almost half its population to death or emigration as a result of the famine.

Famine and Its Aftermath

The winter of 1846–47 was particularly cold and wet in Ireland. The miserable weather and the lack of food soon took their toll on the Irish, who began to die. At first the death count was slight, no more than a trickle. But as the winter wore on and the famine stretched out over months, the trickle increased to a steady flow and finally to a flood.

Starvation was everywhere, and sad stories of suffering filled the pages of local newspapers. This account, printed in the *Cork Examiner* on February 1, 1847, is typical:

> A family of the Cronins, consisting of father, mother, and [son], lived at a place called the Windmill, about a mile from the town of Youghal. On the night of Tuesday last, the mother and her son died in the same bed with the father, whom hunger had rendered so helpless that he could give them no assistance in their last struggle, nor even make their case known to the neighbours. The verdict was death by starvation.

The same article also mentioned the unfortunate Miller family, whose situation was described as "frightful in the extreme. . . . On more than one occasion they had determined to kill and eat the cat, only they feared it would poison them."[60]

Despite the grim conditions, most people had no choice but to sit tight and wait for the famine to lift. A large percentage of these people ultimately died. (The famine would eventually claim nearly 1.5 million lives through starvation and bacterial diseases such as typhus, dysentery, and cholera that often gain a foothold and spread through populations too weakened by hunger to follow adequate sanitation practices.) Other people, however, managed to scrape together enough money to leave the country. More than 2 million Irish fled their homeland during the famine and the years immediately following.

The final toll on the country's population was staggering. Between the emigrants and the blight-related deaths, Ireland lost 3.5 million people—nearly half of the country's prefamine population—over the course of ten years. The population drop was a crippling blow from which Ireland has never fully recovered.

Causes and Control

The potato blight finally receded of its own accord in 1847. Although farmers breathed a collective sigh of relief, the disappearance of the disease was just as much of a mystery as its appearance had been. In fact, the entire episode was a puzzle. What caused the blight? Why did it reach disastrous levels, and why did it end? No one knew.

But these questions were answered in 1861 when scientist Anton de Bary discovered the source of the potato failure. The culprit was a fungus now known as *Phytophthoria infestans*. During cold or dry periods, *P. infestans* does not grow. It lies dormant inside potato plant debris, including old leaves, stems, and tubers. But in warm, wet weather, *P. infestans* resumes its growth, forming countless microscopic spores that are easily carried from one place to another by wind and splashing rain. If the spores land on a damp potato plant, as they did in sixteenth-century Ireland, they burrow in and begin to grow, digesting their host in

Fleeing the Famine

A huge percentage of Ireland's population fled the country during the Great Famine. So many people wanted to leave, in fact, that shipping agents could not provide berths for them all. The situation was described in the April 5, 1847, issue of the *Cork Examiner*.

> The quays are crowded every day with the peasantry from all quarters of the country, who are emigrating to America, both direct from this port and "cross channel" to Liverpool, as the agents here cannot produce enough of ships to convey the people from this unhappy country. . . . When a ship is put on the berth here, she is filled in a day or two, and the agents say if they had 100 ships, they would not be sufficient to meet the demand.

The emigrants hoped to find a better life in a new land—but they paid in suffering for that opportunity. An article in the May 19, 1847, issue of the *New York Sun* included this commentary about shipboard conditions:

> The paupers who have recently arrived from Europe give a most melancholy account of their sufferings. Upwards of eighty individuals, almost dead with the ship fever, were landed from one ship alone, while twenty-seven of the cargo died on the passage, and were thrown into the sea. They were one hundred days tossing to and fro upon the ocean, and for the last twenty days their only food consisted of a few ounces of meal per day, and their only water was obtained from the clouds.

Irish families crowd a quay in hopes of getting aboard a ship bound for America.

This picture depicts potatoes infested with P. infestans, *a fungus that kills the potato plant within a few days.*

the process. The potato plant dies within a few days. By that time, however, the spores have become mature fungi that are able to create and distribute new spores of their own, thus spreading the disease (which today is called late blight) ever outward.

Although *P. infestans* struck Ireland again in 1872 and 1879, the damage was not as severe as it had been during the Great Famine of 1846–47. And in 1890, scientists discovered that fields could be protected from the disease by a chemical called copper sulfate. With that discovery, says George W. Hudler, "the threat of late blight to potatoes and thus to the people who depended on them for food almost disappeared."[61]

Blights Today

But the story doesn't end there. In 1984 a second strain of *P. infestans* was discovered, first in Europe and then in North America. The new fungus was even tougher than the old one, and it could attack tomatoes as well as potatoes. None of the traditional remedies worked well against the new strain of *P. infestans,* which promptly began eating its way through fields of crops. This time there was no famine—but the blight devastated farms and caused sweeping economic damage.

Modern scientists quickly worked out a management program for late blight that combined crop rotation, the burning of diseased plant matter, certified seed inspection, fungicides, and physical barriers. But these techniques could only reduce the disease's impact; they could not stop it altogether. As one scientist

St. Anthony's Fire

Ergot is one common crop-infesting fungus. Ergot does not harm the crop, but it can cause a deadly disease called St. Anthony's Fire in humans who eat the infested foods. In his book *Magical Mushrooms, Mischievous Molds,* fungus expert George W. Hudler describes the causes, effects, and history of this ailment.

Ergot [contains] a wide variety of chemicals known as alkaloids, many of which are hazardous to the health of humans and other animals. One such chemical is ergotamine, a vasoconstrictor powerful enough to completely restrict blood flow to some parts of the body, thus causing a condition known as gangrenous ergotism. Extremities are particularly sensitive, and ergotamine may cause symptoms ranging from the shedding of nails to the loss of hands and feet. In the latter cases, blood-starved limbs simply dry up, turn black, and fall off, with no pain or bleeding. However, the stench associated with the rotting limbs is reported to be overwhelming.

Feelings of intense heat often precede the complete loss of sensation in diseased limbs by several weeks. Thus, some of the earliest references to gangrenous ergotism referred not so much to loss of limbs as to a "plague of fire" or "holy fire.". . . The disease became known as St. Anthony's Fire.

In addition to St. Anthony's Fire, ergot can also cause a disease called convulsive ergotism. Convulsive ergotism is not as deadly as St. Anthony's Fire, but it is far from pleasant, explains Hudler:

Symptoms [range] from vomiting, diarrhea, and general lethargy to a sensation of ants crawling over the body, vivid hallucinations, twitching, grotesque distortion of limbs, and seizures similar to those associated with epilepsy.

said, "A silver bullet for the control of late blight does not exist."[62]
By the year 2000, late blight had made an incredible comeback,
exploding into a worldwide epidemic with an annual monetary
impact exceeding $5 billion.

Between its past and present impacts, *P. infestans* is humankind's most serious fungal enemy. But it is far from the only
one. There are thousands of species of crop-killing fungi, including blights, rusts, smuts, and mildews, in the world, and any one of
these fungi can become an instrument of destruction if it is not
carefully controlled. Farmers therefore use every weapon at their
disposal to prevent harmful fungi from taking hold. The farmers
usually win the battle against known fungal enemies. But sometimes new fungi appear, taking unprepared areas by surprise. Old
enemies may also reappear: As with late blight, a disease that has
been "conquered" occasionally roars back out of nowhere to re-
sume its ravages.

The Monoculture Dilemma

Those ravages, unfortunately, have the potential to be much worse
in the modern world than they ever could have been in ancient
times. The problem lies in an agricultural technique called monoculture.

Monoculture means that every plant in a crop is genetically
identical to every other plant in that same crop. The benefits in
terms of productivity are easy to understand. "By focusing on
a handful of the very best varieties, grain-belt farmers continue
to squeeze ever better harvests from their fields," explains science writer Paul Raeburn. Consumer preferences play an important role, too: "We want the largest, sweetest ears of corn,
the tastiest tomatoes, and the juiciest oranges. Supermarkets
display mountains of uniformly attractive fruits and vegetables. We expect nothing less."[63] Farmers must plant what the
consumers will buy, so they tend to grow just a few favored
species. This pattern has been repeated across the globe in recent decades with the result, says Raeburn, that "Millions of
acres around the world [have] been covered by plants that are
nearly identical."[64]

Monoculture allows farmers to produce genetically identical fruits and vegetables that are larger, tastier, and more attractive.

This modern method is a big change from the traditional one. In earlier times, farmers could not order bags full of genetically identical seeds as they can today. They had to plant whatever they had, which usually meant that they grew many different varieties of a crop at once. A field might contain twenty or thirty different types of beans, for instance. Because many fungi are very specific in their preferences and attack only certain species of plants, this variability provided important protection against crop failure. If two types of beans were destroyed by a blight, well, that was all right; dozens of other strains remained healthy and would keep a farmer fed through the winter.

Thanks to today's perfectly uniform crops, however, that natural buffer is gone. As Raeburn points out, "If a pest finds one cornstalk tasty, it will find them all tasty."[65] The U.S. National Academy of Sciences concurs, calling monoculture "the basis of vulnerability to epidemics."[66] The technique is good in the short term for farmers and consumers—but as far as blights go, it is a disaster waiting to happen.

The Corn Belt Epidemic of 1970

In the mid-1900s, American farmers were unknowingly planting the seeds of just such a disaster.

Since the early years of the century, scientists had been working to develop new and better varieties of corn. The new varieties were called hybrids, and they yielded bigger, tastier ears and kernels than normal corn. Farmers started experimenting with hybrid corn in the 1930s, and they liked the results so well that by the mid-1940s, hybrids had taken over the American corn industry. Fields from Florida to Wisconsin were covered with the new "wonder crop."

But there was a problem. The hybrids' genetic code contained a gap that made the new corn especially vulnerable to certain fungi. In 1970, a fungus later identified as *Bipolaris maydis* found that gap and started to attack hybrid corn crops in southern Florida. The fungus was astonishingly destructive. An environmental consultant explains:

Hybrid corn varieties yield bigger, tastier kernels, but they must be carefully tested to ensure that they do not have hidden vulnerabilities.

Within twenty-four hours it would start making tan, spindle-shaped lesions about an inch long on plant leaves, and in advanced form would attack the stalk, ear shank, husk, kernels, and cob. In extreme infections, whole ears of corn would fall to the ground and crumble at the touch. . . . In its wake, the [fungus] left ravaged corn fields with withered plants, broken stalks, and malformed or completely rotten cobs covered with a grayish powder."[67]

The disease, which came to be known as Southern corn leaf blight, spread like wildfire across America's corn belt. In just four months the fungus traveled from Florida all the way to Canada in the north and Kansas in the west. By the end of September the blight had destroyed 15 percent of America's corn crop, costing farmers about $1 billion. The disease eventually stopped its spread not because of any human efforts, but because of changed weather conditions. In short, the nation got lucky.

The weather was not the only stroke of luck. In terms of human suffering, it was extremely fortunate that the corn leaf blight occurred in a wealthy country with plentiful food supplies. Although the epidemic was financially painful, it did not cause starvation. It is likely, in fact, that most American consumers weren't even aware of the crisis. But as one scientist pointed out at the time, "Such a crop failure in countries such as Guatemala or Kenya, where people obtain half of their calories from corn, would have been disastrous."[68]

Crop Collapse in Samoa

Economic dependence on a single crop can be just as dangerous as nutritional dependence. This truth was demonstrated in the early 1990s when a fungal blight hit the small South Pacific island nation of Samoa. The crop in question was not corn, however, but taro— a starchy vegetable grown in many tropical areas of the world.

Before the blight, taro was Samoa's most important agricultural product. Not only was this plant the main food staple of Samoa's 160,000 residents, it was also one of the country's most profitable exports, bringing in an estimated $3.2 million per year. The nation counted on its annual taro harvest both to feed its citizens and to provide much needed foreign cash. But Samoa's taro had something in common with America's hybrid corn. The taro had what scientists call a narrow genetic base, which means that all of the plants were very similar to each other. And in 1993, that similarity allowed a fungus to wipe out the island's crop.

Lacking America's resources to deal with the problem, the Samoan economy took an immediate nosedive. The country's export earnings plunged, throwing the already poor nation into deeper and deeper debt and creating a recession that affects Samoa to the present day. Tourism is now easing the pain a bit, but the decision to promote tourism was one that would forever change the island nation's character.

The taro blight also had lasting effects on the population's diet. "The experience has prompted farmers to diversify crops extensively to include other agricultural crops such as taamu, yams, cassava, and breadfruit,"[69] reports one organization. And although taro may be making a comeback, progress is slow: "Attempts to develop and adopt disease-resistant varieties [of taro] have not been successful since . . . improved varieties have not been attractive to consumers,"[70] says another organization.

Between the economic and nutritional impacts of the fungus, then, Samoa has changed forever. For this country, taro dependence turned a simple blight into a plague with permanent effects.

Recovering from Disaster

Recovering from an economic disaster is a long, hard process. In Samoa's case, that process has required a great deal of foreign aid. Since the taro failure, Australia, Japan, New Zealand, and other countries have donated many millions of dollars each year to help Samoa's flagging economy. The nation has also racked up significant foreign debt (an estimated $156 million in 1997, the most recent year for which figures are available). Digging out of this economic hole will be difficult at best.

In other countries that experience crop failure, hunger is the bigger problem. Famine-stricken countries can turn to international relief organizations, most notably the United Nations' World Food Programme (WFP), for emergency assistance. Famine relief, however, is a short-term solution. It takes care of immediate needs but doesn't solve the long-term problem. Blights are bound to return if people go right back to the same methods they used before. The WFP therefore works to prevent future disasters by teaching farmers how to fight blights and other crop-destroying pests and pathogens. But this goal is not always realistic in countries where farmers cannot afford effective fungus-control measures.

Farmers in wealthy countries have more options than those in poor countries. They can afford to use state-of-the-art crop protection techniques, with the result that blights do not strike as often. And even if a bad blight does hit, many farmers in America, Canada, and Europe are protected by crop insurance that pays off

World Food Programme (WFP) workers unload bags of food. The WFP not only provides emergency famine relief, but also teaches farmers how to combat future blights.

if a harvest is destroyed. Such insurance makes it much easier for farmers—and their countries—to recover from the devastating effects of crop failure.

Conquering Blights

It would be better, of course, if crop failure never happened in the first place. In the pursuit of this goal, organizations around the world are working to develop new and stronger weapons against blights.

Fungicides, which were first used in the late 1800s, are the most important of these weapons. These chemicals are sprayed or dusted on seeds, leaves, or fruit to prevent the spread of many fungal diseases. In the early days of fungicide use, growers had just a few different chemicals that were applied to every type of crop. But today there are specific narrow-range fungicides for many different purposes, with new ones being introduced all the time. Researchers are also learning ways to apply fungicides for maximum effectiveness.

Fungus-resistant crops are another essential part of the farmer's defense against blights. To develop these crops, scientists called "plant breeders" grow thousands of new strains of plants, then test each one to see if it has inborn defenses against fungi. Those that do are crossbred with other resistant plants. The process is repeated over and over until the plant breeders have created a new species that is tough enough to stop fungi in the real world. Once established in a farmer's field, these crops provide excellent protection against blights and other dangerous diseases.

Fungicide application, crop breeding programs, and a handful of other techniques have revolutionized the field of agriculture. The new methods have all but conquered a number of dangerous blights, removing some of the farming community's biggest worries. Many blights are still a problem—but with today's knowledge, these diseases can usually be controlled to varying degrees. All in all, it is fair to say that the modern farmer is in a much better position than his historical counterpart.

A Delicate Balance

But the balance of power is a delicate one, and constant attention is required to keep it tipped in humankind's favor. Beating blights is never an easy task—and as the on-again, off-again threat of *P. infestans* clearly shows, even victory cannot be taken for granted. Farmers and scientists are therefore locked into a perpetual struggle with fungal plant diseases. They must fight at all times to stay one step ahead of disaster.

One problem is that fungus-resistant plants don't stay that way forever. As Paul Raeburn explains:

Resistance is a fleeting thing. It is a game of leapfrog between breeders and predators. Breeders produce a new crop variety that resists common pests and diseases. Within a few years, an insect or microbe mutates. It acquires the ability to overcome the resistance. . . . Breeders respond with a variety that is resistant to the new predator. Farmers gain a few more years. Then the cycle repeats.[71]

Each cycle, according to Raeburn, has a lifetime of about seven years, a period barely sufficient to allow plant breeders to do their work.

There are problems with fungicides, too. Some of the most effective fungicides have been banned in recent years because of their potentially harmful effects on people, animals, and the environment. And although many good fungicides are still available, they will become less and less powerful over time as fungi evolve and develop resistance. Chemical companies around the world are working to create new fungicides to fill the coming gaps.

An Irish farmer sprays pesticides over a potato field to prevent an outbreak of potato blight. Unfortunately, fungicides are only temporarily effective since fungi evolve and eventually develop resistance to the chemicals.

But the biggest problem of all is the continuing spread of mono-culture, which may well turn out to be agriculture's Achilles' heel. Acres upon acres of genetically identical plants are, in the words of one scientist, "like a tinder-dry prairie waiting for a spark to ignite it."[72] That spark could be an unknown fungus, or it could be an old one that has found chinks in humankind's defenses. The battle to identify and prevent the spark will be difficult, for as George W. Hudler points out, "Fungi, especially the troublesome ones, just do not give up."[73]

Plague Prevention . . . and Its Consequences

As far as humans are concerned, plagues are disastrous. Epidemics and famines have killed untold millions of people; swarms and blights have driven countless more into ruin. Families are torn apart, industries collapse, and economies fail under the plague's assault.

The natural perspective, however, is very different from the human one. From nature's viewpoint, a disease that wipes out 25 million people is no disaster. It is simply an indication that some imbalance has occurred, allowing the disease-causing microorganism to run rampant. Disease outbreaks are natural processes intended to restore balance, as are swarms, bioinvasions, and blights.

Although people have always fought these natural processes to the best of their ability, only in recent centuries have they enjoyed significant success. Humankind now knows how to overcome many dangerous diseases, bring some swarms under control, and increase crop security worldwide, to name just a few advances.

This situation is good for humans. But it is not so good for nature, perhaps. Plague control efforts interrupt the processes that restore balance to the earth. Nature resists these efforts—and the results are sometimes surprising. Human attempts at plague control have had some damaging and even potentially deadly consequences.

Man vs. Nature

Until recently, humans were poorly equipped to fight plagues. Farmers, for example, had no chemicals to kill marauding bugs.

Instead, they had to rely on physical barriers and human labor to stop insect invasions. They dug long furrows to block marching creatures from entering their fields, and they spent weary hours hand-plucking beetles and grubs from plants. These techniques sometimes worked, but as author Gilbert Waldbauer relates, "People were more often than not helpless when faced by an insect attack. The arrival of a large swarm of migratory locusts, for example, was an unmitigated disaster. . . . Farmers burned them with torches and smashed them with brooms and spades, but the locusts kept coming. It was like trying to drain a river with a bucket."[74]

Farmers were equally helpless against most invasive weeds. Some of the invaders could be controlled by techniques such as hand-pulling, deep plowing, and crop rotation. But the struggle was constant and difficult. If a weed was edible, farmers sometimes just gave up the fight and started growing the plant on purpose. Oats, radishes, lettuces, beets, and leeks, all of which probably started out as weeds, stand today as hard evidence of nature's triumph over man.

Early attempts to control pestilence were also ineffective, mostly because they were based on incorrect assumptions about how dis-

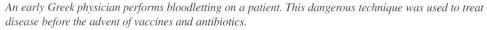

An early Greek physician performs bloodletting on a patient. This dangerous technique was used to treat disease before the advent of vaccines and antibiotics.

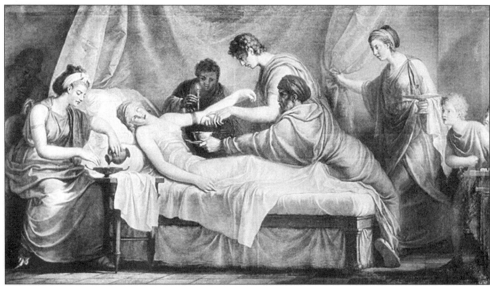

eases worked. Many ancient civilizations blamed their troubles on gods and spirits, with the result that prayer, sacrifices, and other appeals to the supernatural were the preferred treatments for any ailment. But while these measures may have been comforting, they had little medical effect. Doctors eventually began to suspect that diseases had a physical cause, but some of their cures—including bloodletting and the amputation of affected body parts—were worse than the disease itself. Other techniques were harmless but didn't do much good, either. Because of its medical ignorance, humankind was basically helpless in the face of a major epidemic.

Triumph over Disease

But the medical situation changed dramatically in the mid-1940s when vaccines, antibiotics, and other discoveries revolutionized world health care. Due to these advances, "Infection's oppressive grip on human health changed radically, at least in developed countries," notes author Jason Eberhart-Phillips. He continues:

> Antibiotics were performing like invincible "magic bullets" against . . . fatal bacterial diseases. Vaccines were reinventing the experience of childhood, emancipating children from epidemics of whooping cough and measles and protecting them from the paralyzing effects of polio. Smallpox . . . was well on its way to being wiped off the earth. It was an exultant time for public health, as one miracle seemed to follow another. [75]

Thanks to the new medicines and technologies, fewer people contracted serious diseases, and those who did were much more likely to recover. The childhood death rate plummeted and human life expectancy rose. By the mid-1950s, medical professionals around the globe were declaring victory in the war against infectious disease. "It is hardly too much to say that infectious disease has now ceased to have any serious social significance in the advanced countries of the world," [76] stated a 1953 medical textbook. And within a few years, even then U.S. surgeon general William H. Stewart was ready to confirm this view: "It is time to close the book on infectious diseases [and] declare the war against pestilence won," [77] he said in a 1970 appearance before Congress.

A geneticist sprays a Bt solution on tomato plants to determine its toxicity to the Colorado potato beetle.

Mastering Microbes

Humans used their newfound mastery over microbes not only to prevent and cure diseases, but also to conquer other old enemies.

One major success in this field involved the deliberate spread of myxomatosis, a viral disease of rabbits. In 1950 the virus that causes myxomatosis was released in southeastern Australia in an attempt to control the continent's rabbit invasion. The disease took hold and began to spread across Australia in a deadly wave, killing 99 percent of its intended victims. Within two years the continent's rabbit population had dropped from 600 million to less than 100 million, bringing the worst of the infestation to an end. Although rabbits are still a pest species in Australia, their population has never again exploded to plague numbers and probably never will, since myxomatosis has become endemic across the continent.

Bacteria, too, were to prove useful in the war against plagues. Scientists discovered, for instance, that certain naturally occurring bacteria can kill insect pests. One example is *Bacillus thuringiensis*, usually called Bt. Bt is most often dusted onto crops in powder form; it may also be genetically incorporated into the plant itself. After Bt is eaten by a bug, it produces deadly toxins that quickly kill the host insect. Yet this microbe does no harm to plants, humans, animals, or insects other than its target victim, making it an ideal control agent.

Scientists also discovered that bacteria could protect crops against fungi. Seeds could be coated with protective microbes that kept fungi from attacking, for example. Harmless soilborne bacteria could use up certain nutrients that fungi needed, thus keeping the invaders at bay. And some bacteria would even attack and consume unfriendly fungi. These and other microbial control techniques continue to have major impacts on world agriculture.

Stopping Pests

Modern pesticides (including insecticides, fungicides, and herbicides) had an even greater effect.

Although primitive pesticides had been used for centuries, it wasn't until the 1940s that really effective chemicals were developed. The new pesticides were efficient killers, quickly slaying troublesome weeds, fungi, and insects. DDT, a powerful insecticide, was just one of the many impressive chemicals that became available to farmers at this time. Author V. G. Dethier describes the laboratory discovery of this insecticide: "[It] had remarkable properties. Minute amounts were lethal not only to lice, but also

Farmers use a special tractor to spray hybrid cornfields with DDT in 1946. A variety of powerful pesticides became available to farmers in the 1940s.

to mosquitoes, bed bugs, fleas, flies, and indeed to nearly every insect. At one point, a small amount of the chemical accidentally blown into the air almost destroyed the entire colony of yellow-fever mosquitoes in the laboratory."[78]

DDT and other pesticides were not only incredibly effective, they were also inexpensive. Farmers had a new arsenal at their disposal and they used it liberally. The results were dramatic and immediate. Some insect pests were brought under control for the first time in human history. The boll weevil is one example: "Using carefully timed pesticide applications, farmers have nearly eradicated the cotton boll weevil in large areas of the southeast; this pest devastated the cotton-based southern farm economy at the beginning of the twentieth century,"[79] writes scientist Keith S. Delaplane. Fungicides wiped out once devastating plant diseases. And herbicides protected fields from weeds, with a resulting increase in crop yield: "Worldwide, herbicides have provided a 10- to 20-percent increase in bread grains, enough for 15 loaves of bread for each person on the earth,"[80] according to Delaplane.

Modern pesticides did not just make life easier for farmers. They changed the world. In the United States alone, Delaplane explains, "These chemicals improve food quality, quantity, and variety. They improve human health by controlling natural food poisons, increasing production of fruits and vegetables, and helping to control long-forgotten diseases. They protect our homes and property."[81] Humankind today enjoys many advantages, Delaplane points out, that are the direct result of pesticide usage.

The First Signs of Trouble

Between the effects of pesticides and medical advances, it seemed that humankind had finally gained the upper hand over many plagues. The result was a brief, shining era during which optimism ran rampant in the scientific community. Medical professionals began referring to "a post-infection era." Entomologists, not content merely to control insects, began plotting the total and permanent eradication of all bugs, everywhere. And farmers stopped worrying about fungi and weeds. They simply dusted their crops with pesticides on a regular schedule and trusted science to protect them from disaster.

The New Killers

Here is a snapshot of a few frightening human diseases that have erupted since the mid-1970s.

Ebola Hemorrhagic Fever—Epidemics have occurred in the African countries of Sudan, Gabon, and the Congo. The disease starts with a fever, muscle pains, headache, and sore throat. Within a few days, victims begin bleeding from every orifice and their internal organs start to disintegrate. Death follows in nearly 90 percent of all cases.

Hantavirus Pulmonary Syndrome—Outbreaks of this acute respiratory illness have occurred all over the world. The illness at first causes fevers and aches. It soon moves into the lungs, filling the chest with fluid and causing its victims to drown in their own secretions.

Hemorrhagic Colitis—This illness occurs when a person eats food that is contaminated with a new and dangerous form of the bacterium *E. coli*. The infection causes severe abdominal cramps and bloody diarrhea. Most sufferers recover without treatment, but a few people die from this ailment every year.

Legionnaires' Disease—This "killer pneumonia," as it has been called, occurs when tiny water droplets carrying a deadly bacterium are inhaled. Outbreaks of Legionnaires' Disease have been traced to contaminated hot tubs and air conditioning systems. Scientists estimate that this ailment kills two thousand to six thousand people each year.

Lyme Disease—Transmitted by the bite of a tick, this disease causes fever, fatigue, headaches, and persistent joint pain. In some people the symptoms can last for years and may progress to include impaired memory, meningitis, or paralysis.

Variant Creutzfeldt-Jakob Disease—The human form of bovine spongiform encephalopathy, popularly called Mad Cow Disease. Victims suffer memory loss and other mental problems as well as movement and balance problems. There is no known treatment for vCJD. So far, all patients have died.

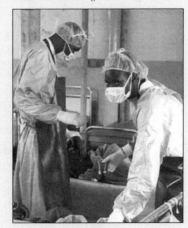

Medical workers help victims of the Ebola virus in Uganda.

But the first signs of trouble appeared in the 1970s, when new diseases began to emerge. Some of these diseases were deadly, and most were proving difficult or even impossible to cure. Even more distressing was the fact that "conquered" diseases such as cholera, malaria, and diphtheria were making a comeback. By the 1980s, says one scientist, it had become evident that "Humanity's enemies in the microscopic world were not about to accept an unconditional surrender."[82]

Many factors contributed to the emergence of new diseases and the reemergence of old ones. Most alarming to medical professionals, however, was the fact that microbes were becoming resistant to the new wonder drugs. A simple process was at work: "Infectious organisms, like all living things, evolve over generations to adapt to new circumstances . . . [and] due to their immense numbers and rates of reproduction, bacteria and viruses can run the evolutionary race at breakneck speed,"[83] explains Jason Eberhart-Phillips. Antibiotics and other medicines killed virtually all harmful microbes—but some especially hardy individuals survived and reproduced, creating a new and stronger generation of microbes. Over the course of several decades this process produced "super bugs" that were able to resist any treatment doctors could throw at them.

Humankind's heavy use of antibiotics is directly responsible for this situation, which looks increasingly dire. The problem has gotten bad enough that today, says Eberhart-Phillips, "Doctors are voicing genuine fears that soon they may be powerless to stop bacteria and other pathogens. . . . Some doctors even speculate that a 'post-antibiotic era' waits in the wings, when humanity is laid waste by a host of invincible bacterial adversaries, as it was in centuries past."[84]

Trouble on the Farm

Just as medicines are becoming less effective against some diseases, insecticides are losing their ability to kill certain bugs—and for much the same reasons. Indiscriminate spraying of powerful insecticides such as DDT kills most pests, but leaves the toughest ones alive to reproduce. The eventual result is a generation of fully resistant insects that are impossible to con-

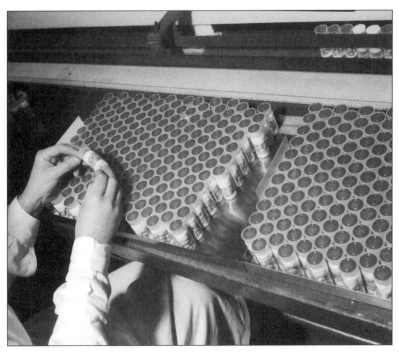

An assembly-line worker fills bottles of antibiotics. The world's heavy use of antibiotics has produced "super bugs" that are completely resistant to treatment.

trol through once effective methods. The chilling potential of this situation is illustrated by the words of science writer V. G. Dethier: "Nothing can bring the problem home more forcefully than to visit a laboratory where cultures of resistant varieties are kept for study, and to observe a thriving colony of flies living in a cage coated solidly with DDT."[85]

Fungi and invasive plants may also develop resistance to specific pesticides over time, with sometimes devastating results. The 1984 reappearance of late blight provides a troubling example of this reality. In the late 1970s a chemical called metalaxyl was introduced to control *P. infestans*, the fungus responsible for late blight. Although the new fungicide worked well for a decade or so, *P. infestans* soon developed resistance to metalaxyl and resumed its destruction of potato and tomato crops around the world. Lacking an effective fungicide to fight the disease, farmers today take a multipronged approach to late blight control that combines several less-than-ideal solutions and which sometimes falls short of success. Scientists hope for eventual victory, but the outcome of this particular fight is far from certain. "The disease is going to be much more difficult to control than it used to be,"[86] sighs one plant pathologist.

Pesticide resistance is not the only problem farmers face. Humankind's chemical assault on pests has had many unexpected consequences, some of which have actually made the original problem worse. Some insecticides, for example, kill *all* insects, not just their target victims. The mass slaughter of a region's insect ecosystem temporarily eliminates harmful pests, but it also clears the way for new invasions. Why? "[Some insecticides] kill so many beneficial insects that the parasites and predators that normally keep other insects from becoming pests are removed from the ecosystem," explains Dethier. As a result, "Insects and other arthropods that [have] never before bothered growers [become] destructive overnight."[87]

The Prevention Cycle

Pesticide resistance and other negative consequences of chemical pest control have created an ever escalating prevention cycle. Farmers apply pesticides to control insects, weeds, and fungi. The pests eventually overcome the controls and become even more difficult to subdue. The farmers apply different, stronger, or greater quantities of pesticides to keep their crops safe. And then the cycle repeats itself. It is a never-ending battle—and one that some experts say humankind is losing. For example, "Insecticide use on all U.S. crops has increased tenfold since 1945. At the same time, crop losses have nearly doubled, from 7 percent to 13 percent,"[88] writes Paul Raeburn. From a percentage perspective, losses are actually greater today than they were before pesticides were introduced.

But although pest losses are increasing, so are crop yields. Farmers today expect a field to produce about double the harvest it did a few decades ago. While pesticides are not solely responsible for this increase, they do play a critical role. Without them, food supplies would plummet and people around the world would be plunged into famine. Farmers therefore have little choice but to continue the prevention cycle and hope that they can stay in the lead.

Medical professionals face the same issues, particularly in their war against harmful bacteria. Antibiotic-resistant microbes are forcing doctors to use new varieties and increased quantities of drugs to cure sick patients. This strategy is mostly working—for now. But as with pesticide use, there is a cycle at work. Each medical innovation is answered by a microbial adaptation. There is no way around this fact. As one scientist says, "The action of antibiotics and resistance to these drugs are linked like light and shadow: One does not exist without the other."[89]

Biological Control

So it is becoming increasingly clear that human-engineered controls can have dangerous side effects. Scientists and world leaders are therefore experimenting with natural control methods that they hope will be effective, yet have fewer damaging consequences.

Despite the negative consequences of pesticide use, chemical pest control efforts have increased tenfold since 1945.

One much-talked-about method is biological control, or bio-control for short. This approach involves the manipulation of the environment to produce conditions that are natural, but unfavorable to an invader. The release of myxomatosis during the Australian rabbit infestation is a good example of a successful biological control effort. Myxomatosis was a natural disease, already endemic in some parts of the world. It therefore provoked no "counterattack" from nature. And yet it was superbly effective, bringing the rabbit plague under control in a matter of years without any unintended consequences.

Another biocontrol effort is currently underway in the U.S. Great Lakes, which have been overrun with invading sea lampreys since the mid-1940s. Scientists are finding the lampreys' mating sites and releasing thousands of sterilized males into the waters. The natural mating cycle occurs without interruption—but the females are unable to produce viable eggs, with the result that the next generation of lampreys is greatly reduced. No pesticides are involved, so there is no danger of a resistance buildup or unintended ecological harm.

So in certain situations, biocontrol can be both safe and effective. But it can also go awry, as it did in the case of the snail *Euglandina rosea* (also called the rosy wolfsnail). This creature was deliberately introduced into many Pacific islands in the 1950s as a natural control for the giant African snail, a crop and garden pest. *Euglandina* did prey upon the African snails. But it turned out that *Euglandina* liked the islands' smaller snails even better. Within a short period the introduced "biocontrol agent" had exterminated hundreds of species of beautiful and harmless snails throughout the Pacific region.

The disastrous *Euglandina* experiment was one of many hard lessons that scientists have learned about using biocontrol wisely. As one scientist says, "Conservation is full of sad stories, but there can be few sadder than this, the totally unnecessary and pointless destruction of fascinating biodiversity by a deliberate introduction. . . . It is the sharpest reminder that biocontrol must be absolutely specific (and remain so) to be safe."[90]

Before flea beetles are released in the United States as biocontrol insects, an entomologist studies the effect they have on a variety of different crops and plants.

Overcoming Obstacles

Both natural and artificial plague controls, then, can have significant pitfalls—and new problems keep appearing. Far from giving up, however, humans are fighting harder than ever to develop new ways to cope with pestilence, swarms, bioinvaders, and blights.

On the agricultural front, many farmers are fighting pests through a fairly new process called integrated pest management (IPM). IPM combines careful monitoring of an area's pest population with chemical, biological, and physical controls. The program aims to control pests while reducing the use of potentially harmful or resistance-producing pesticides. Over time it is hoped that IPM techniques will enable farmers to cut their pesticide use by as much as 50 percent.

On the medical front, scientists are combing the world's rain forests, seas, and other remote areas to find new and perhaps medically useful substances. Worldwide campaigns have been launched to reduce the casual use of antibiotics and thus to slow the emergence of resistant bacteria. And massive educational programs are underway around the globe to teach people how to protect themselves

The Downward Spiral of Biocontrol

Biological control can be effective against invasive species. If it is not used carefully, however, it may set off an unexpected and damaging chain of events. In his book *Life out of Bounds: Bioinvasion in a Borderless World*, research scientist Chris Bright describes the downward spiral that occurred on the islands of Micronesia after an attempt at rat biocontrol.

The effort began by importing giant monitor lizards. But rats are active at night; they are not suitable prey for the monitors, which are active during the day. So the monitors turned to poultry instead. Sometime before 1945, an enormous South American toad, called the cane toad, was imported to give the monitors something else to eat and perhaps also to keep down insects in the coconut plantations.

The toad secretes a powerful venom from its skin, and large numbers of monitors were poisoned. As the monitors died off, one of the coconut pests, a rhinoceros beetle, underwent a population explosion because the monitors had been eating its grubs. With the monitors out of the way, the toad population exploded too. Cats, dogs, and pigs attacked the toads and were killed in their turn. Then the rat population exploded because the cats and dogs had been preying on the rats. The giant African snail, brought in by the Japanese during World War II as a food, exploded as well, perhaps partly because of all the available carrion in the form of cat and dog carcasses. During the 1970s and 1980s, a predatory flatworm was introduced to try to control the snail. The flatworm is currently spreading throughout the islands and has become a major new threat to Oceania's extraordinarily diverse native snail fauna.

from humankind's most common diseases. AIDS and other incurable illnesses will be brought under control, it is hoped, when people everywhere understand how to avoid them.

And on the bioinvasion front, increased vigilance and stricter import regulations are the watchwords of the day. Because the scope of the world bioinvasion problem has only recently been acknowledged, however, control efforts are still in their infancy. It is unclear how successful these efforts will be or how bad the problem will become before controls are devised, if indeed this turns out to be possible.

Looking to the Future

No matter how good human control efforts become, the plague problem will never go away. Individual plagues may be conquered—the eradication of smallpox is proof that such small-scale success is possible—but new plagues inevitably will pop up to take the place of those that have disappeared. This fact is reflected in scientists' attitudes, which in recent decades have shifted from smug triumph to cautious optimism and finally to a resigned acceptance of plagues as a fact of life on earth. There is a growing recognition that nature will eventually have its way, no matter what barriers are placed in its path.

It is likely, in fact, that humankind's plague problem will get worse rather than better. The reason lies in the earth's exploding human population, which now numbers more than 6 billion individuals and is projected to reach 10 to 12 billion before leveling off. An incredible natural imbalance is being created by this massive influx of human beings, and their accompanying agriculture, cities, pollution, and other disruptions. Inevitably, nature will react as human activities continue to bring about far-reaching and often unanticipated changes. And until a new balance is reached, humankind will undoubtedly be subjected to unpredictable and increasingly frequent plagues.

It is possible that these plagues will also do increasing damage. Humankind's newfound global mobility has made it possible for a dread disease or a deadly crop blight to travel around the world before its presence is even noticed. Because the spreading-out process is so easy, scientists fear that a plague could strike with an intensity never before experienced in human history.

So the global community watches and waits, keeping at hand its medicines, its pesticides, its educational tools, and its technologies. But despite humankind's impressive arsenal, the ages-old questions remain. Where will the plague come from? What form will it take? How much damage will it do? And most important of all: What can individuals do to minimize the impact of the inevitable?

Notes

Chapter 1: Pestilence

1. James Cross Giblin, *When Plague Strikes*. New York: HarperCollins, 1995, pp. 11–12.
2. Giblin, *When Plague Strikes*, p. 16.
3. Quoted in Dr. E. L. Skip Knox, "The Black Death," *ORB (The Online Reference Book for Medieval Studies)*. orb.rhodes.edu/textbooks/westciv/blackdeath.html.
4. Giblin, *When Plague Strikes*, p. 19.
5. Ron Wild, "The Black Death," *History Magazine*, October/November 1999. www.history-magazine.com/black.html.
6. Knox, "The Black Death."
7. World Health Organization, "Tuberculosis Fact Sheet." www.who.int/inf-fs/en/fact104.html.
8. Randy Bird and Garland E. Allen, "Louis Pasteur," Microsoft *Encarta*, 1994. CD-ROM.
9. World Health Organization, "Achievements and Challenges." www.who.int/aboutwho/en/achievements.html.
10. Brent Hoff and Carter Smith III, *Mapping Epidemics: A Historical Atlas of Disease*. New York: Franklin Watts, 2000, p. 38.
11. Hoff and Smith, *Mapping Epidemics*, p. 39.
12. UNAIDS, "Best Practice Summary Booklet: Introduction to Antiretroviral Therapy." www.unaids.org/bestpractice/collection/subject/care/antiretroviral.html.
13. UNAIDS, "Best Practice Summary Booklet."

14. Johanna McGeary, "Death Stalks a Continent," *Time*, February 12, 2001. www.time.com.

15. Jason Eberhart-Phillips, M.D., *Outbreak Alert*. Oakland, CA: New Harbinger Publications, 2000, p. 11.

16. Quoted in Kathleen McAuliffe, "The Killing Fields: Latter-Day Plagues," *Omni*, May 1990. SIRS Knowledge Source. sks.sirs.com.

17. Quoted in Eberhart-Phillips, *Outbreak Alert*, p. 11.

Chapter 2: Swarms

18. Quoted in Gilbert Waldbauer, *Millions of Monarchs, Bunches of Beetles*. Cambridge, MA: Harvard University Press, 2000, pp. 138–39.

19. Quoted in Nevard Family Website, "Eyewitness Accounts of Locust-Swarms." members.tripod.com/~NevFam2/material/locust.htm.

20. Quoted in Waldbauer, *Millions of Monarchs, Bunches of Beetles*, pp. 135–36.

21. U.S. Office of Technology Assessment (OTA), "A Plague of Locusts," June 1990, p. 9.

22. OTA, "A Plague of Locusts," pp. 15–16.

23. OTA, "A Plague of Locusts," p. 10.

24. Waldbauer, *Millions of Monarchs, Bunches of Beetles*, p. 146.

25. R. A. Bell, "The Army Worm and Kikuyu Poisoning," Kwazulu-Natal Department of Agriculture and Environmental Affairs. agriculture.kzntl.gov.za/publications/books/kikuyu_technology_day/kikuyu_page19.htm.

26. Zai Whitaker, "Winning the Rat Race in India," *International Wildlife*, November/December 1992. SIRS Knowledge Source. sks.sirs.com.

27. Bret Wallach, *At Odds with Progress: Americans and Conservation*. Tucson: University of Arizona Press, 1991. Posted on the University of Oklahoma Geography Department's website. geography.ou.edu/research/aowp2.html.

28. Sue Hubbell, "In Missouri: The Cicada's Song," *Time*, July 15, 1985.

29. Quoted in Ohio Lake Erie Commission, "101 Uses for a Mayfly?" *North Coast Newsletter*, September/October 2000, p. 4.

30. Quoted in John Seewer, "Swarm of Annoyance: Lake Erie Insects Arrive," *Cincinnati Enquirer*, July 3, 2000. enquirer.com/editions/2000/07/03/loc_swarm_of_annoyance.html.

31. Quoted in Steve Grant, "A Bug's Lifeline," *Hartford Courant*, September 14, 1999. SIRS Knowledge Source. sks.sirs.com.

32. Quoted in Grant, "A Bug's Lifeline."

33. Ohio Lake Erie Commission, "101 Uses for a Mayfly?" p. 4.

34. Quoted in Australian Nature Live Answer Sheet. www.users. bigpond.com/cassowary/answers.htm.

35. OTA, "A Plague of Locusts," p. 16.

Chapter 3: Bioinvasion

36. Chris Bright, *Life out of Bounds: Bioinvasion in a Borderless World*. New York: W. W. Norton, 1998, p. 19.

37. Chris Bright, "Bio-Invasions: The Spread of Exotic Species," *World Watch*, July/August 1995. SIRS Knowledge Source. sks.sirs.com.

38. U.S. Office of Technology Assessment, "Harmful Non-Indigenous Species in the United States," September 1993, p. 5.

39. Bright, *Life out of Bounds*, p. 139.

40. Shelly Parer, "History of the European Wild Rabbit in Australia." rubens.anu.edu.au/student.projects/rabbits/history.html.

41. Parer, "History of the European Wild Rabbit in Australia."

42. Parer, "History of the European Wild Rabbit in Australia."

43. Bright, *Life out of Bounds*, p. 157.

44. Quoted in Patricia Leigh Brown, "The Plague of New Orleans," *New York Times*, May 14, 2000. www.nytimes. com/learning/students/pop/051400sci-animal-termite.html.

45. Brown, "The Plague of New Orleans."

46. Quoted in Brown, "The Plague of New Orleans."

47. Andrew C. Revkin, "March of the Fire Ants," *Discover*, March 1989. SIRS Knowledge Source. sks.sirs.com.

48. Dana Cole, "California's Urbanizing Wetlands and 'The Fire of the Future,'" Information Center for the Environment. www.ice.ucdavis.edu/cafe/agenda97/FireManagement/ Planning/8FMCole.html.

49. National Fire Protection Association, "The Oakland/Berkeley Hills Fire of 1991." www.firewise.org/pubs/theOakland BerkeleyHillsFire/abstract.html.

50. Quoted in Revkin, "March of the Fire Ants."

51. Daniel Simberloff, "Impacts of Introduced Species in the United States," *Consequences,* vol. 2, no. 2, 1996. U.S. Global Change Research Information Office. www.gcrio.org/ CONSEQUENCES/vol2no2/article2.html.

52. Simberloff, "Impacts of Introduced Species in the United States."

53. Quoted in Revkin, "March of the Fire Ants."

54. Ronald Bailey, "Bio Invaders!" *Reason*, August/September 2000. SIRS Knowledge Source. sks.sirs.com.

55. Chris Reuther, "Invaders from Earth," Academy of Natural Sciences, May 1999. www.acnatsci.org/erd/ea/exotics.html.

56. Bailey, "Bio Invaders!"

Chapter 4: Blights

57. George W. Hudler, *Magical Mushrooms, Mischievous Molds.* Princeton, NJ: Princeton University Press, 1998, p. 36.

58. Hudler, *Magical Mushrooms, Mischievous Molds*, p. 36.

59. Quoted in Hudler, *Magical Mushrooms, Mischievous Molds*, p. 37.

60. Uncredited author, "Deaths by Starvation," *Cork Examiner*, February 1, 1847. View of the Famine. vassun.vassar.edu/ ~sttaylor/FAMINE/Examiner/Archives/Feb1847.html.

61. Hudler, *Magical Mushrooms, Mischievous Molds,* p. 43.

62. Phil Arneson, "Late Blight: Management of the Epidemic," author's website. arneson.cornell.edu/Olplpath/Profiles/Lateblit/Pa2307t0.htm.

63. Paul Raeburn, *The Last Harvest.* New York: Simon & Schuster, 1995, p. 12.

64. Raeburn, *The Last Harvest,* p. 12.

65. Raeburn, *The Last Harvest,* p. 13.

66. Jack Doyle, *Altered Harvest.* New York: Viking Press, 1985. Unsafe Science. www.un-safescience.com/cms-sclb.html.

67. Quoted in Doyle, *Altered Harvest.*

68. Quoted in Doyle, *Altered Harvest.*

69. Food & Agriculture Organization, "Foodcrops & Shortages: Samoa," October 2000. www.fao.org/giews/english/fs/fs0010/pays/sam0010e.htm.

70. International Plant Genetic Resources Institute, "TaroGen: Improving Nutrition and Incomes Through Taro Research," PGR-2, June 2000. www.ipgri.cgiar.org/pgr/pgr.asp?nb=2.

71. Raeburn, *The Last Harvest,* p. 13.

72. Quoted in Doyle, *Altered Harvest.*

73. Hudler, *Magical Mushrooms, Mischievous Molds,* pp. 50–51.

Chapter 5: Plague Prevention . . . and Its Consequences
74. Waldbauer, *Millions of Monarchs, Bunches of Beetles,* p. 159.

75. Eberhart-Phillips, *Outbreak Alert,* pp. 6–7

76. Quoted in Eberhart-Phillips, *Outbreak Alert,* p. 7.

77. World Health Organization, "WHO Report on Global Surveillance of Epidemic-Prone Infectious Diseases," 2000, p. 1.

78. V. G. Dethier, *Man's Plague? Insects and Agriculture.* Princeton, NJ: Darwin Press, 1976, p. 112.

79. Keith S. Delaplane, "Pesticide Usage in the United States: History, Benefits, Risks, and Trends," University of Georgia College of Agricultural & Environmental Services. www.ces.uga.edu/pubcd/B1121.htm.

80. Delaplane, "Pesticide Usage in the United States."

81. Delaplane, "Pesticide Usage in the United States."

82. Eberhart-Phillips, *Outbreak Alert*, p. 8.

83. Eberhart-Phillips, *Outbreak Alert*, p. 163.

84. Eberhart-Phillips, *Outbreak Alert*, p. 183.

85. Dethier, *Man's Plague?* p. 119.

86. Quoted in Raeburn, *The Last Harvest*, p. 147.

87. Dethier, *Man's Plague?* p. 119.

88. Raeburn, *The Last Harvest*, p. 209.

89. Quoted in Eberhart-Phillips, *Outbreak Alert*, p. 191.

90. Mark Williamson, *Biological Invasions*. London: Chapman & Hall, 1996, pp. 148–49.

For Further Reading

Linda Jacobs Altman, *Plague and Pestilence: A History of Infectious Disease.* Springfield, NJ: Enslow, 1998. A good summary of the major events in the history of infectious disease.

Virginia Aronson, *The Influenza Pandemic of 1918.* Philadelphia: Chelsea House, 2000. An exploration of the Spanish flu pandemic, from its earliest days to its eventual retreat.

Rodney Barker, *And the Waters Turned to Blood.* New York: Simon & Schuster, 1997. A dramatic true account of the U.S. scientific community's efforts to halt the spread of *Pfiesteria piscicida,* a microorganism that causes deadly HABs.

Michael J. Novacek, ed., *The Biodiversity Crisis: Losing What Counts.* New York: The New Press, 2001. An easy-to-read explanation of the wave of extinction currently occurring all over the earth. Biodiversity reduction is an ecological aspect of the bioinvasion problem.

Richard Preston, *The Hot Zone.* New York: Anchor Books, 1995. Contains dramatic but true stories of several deadly disease outbreaks that occurred between 1967 and 1993.

Works Consulted

Books

Chris Bright, *Life out of Bounds: Bioinvasion in a Borderless World*. New York: W. W. Norton, 1998. The author of this book is one of the top names in the field of bioinvasion. The text is interesting, informative, and highly readable.

Robert Browning, *The Pied Piper of Hamelin*. London: Frederick Warne, 1888. This famous children's book tells the classic fairy tale of the Pied Piper.

V. G. Dethier, *Man's Plague? Insects and Agriculture*. Princeton, NJ: Darwin Press, 1976. Examines the insect threat to agriculture and man's response to that threat.

Jason Eberhart-Phillips, M.D., *Outbreak Alert*. Oakland, CA: New Harbinger Publications, 2000. An examination of the important topics surrounding infectious diseases. The book is packed with good information about diseases that have emerged since 1980.

James Cross Giblin, *When Plague Strikes*. New York: Harper-Collins, 1995. Contains detailed histories of three major plagues: the Black Death, smallpox, and AIDS.

Brent Hoff and Carter Smith III, *Mapping Epidemics: A Historical Atlas of Disease*. New York: Franklin Watts, 2000. Summarizes the causes, symptoms, treatment, and histories of the major human infectious diseases.

George W. Hudler, *Magical Mushrooms, Mischievous Molds.* Princeton, NJ: Princeton University Press, 1998. All about fungi, including their structure, functions, and effects. Includes many interesting case studies of fungi that attack crops and humans.

Andrew Lang, ed., *The Red Fairy Book.* London: Longmans, Green, 1891. A good source for little-known versions of traditional fairy tales.

Paul Raeburn, *The Last Harvest.* New York: Simon & Schuster, 1995. A fascinating examination of modern threats to world agriculture.

Gilbert Waldbauer, *Millions of Monarchs, Bunches of Beetles.* Cambridge, MA: Harvard University Press, 2000. This engaging book examines the causes and effects of insect swarms. Includes many interesting case studies.

Mark Williamson, *Biological Invasions.* London: Chapman & Hall, 1996. A scientific examination of the world bioinvasion problem.

Internet Sources

Phil Arneson, "Late Blight: Management of the Epidemic," author's website. arneson.cornell.edu/Olplpath/Profiles/Lateblit/Pa2307t0.htm.

Australian Nature Live Answer Sheet. www.users.bigpond.com/cassowary/answers.htm.

Ronald Bailey, "Bio Invaders!" *Reason*, August/September 2000. SIRS Knowledge Source. sks.sirs.com.

R. A. Bell, "The Army Worm and Kikuyu Poisoning," Kwazulu-Natal Department of Agriculture and Environmental Affairs website. agriculture.kzntl.gov.za/publications/books/kikuyu_technology_day/kikuyu_page19.htm.

Randy Bird and Garland E. Allen, "Louis Pasteur," Microsoft *Encarta*, 1994. CD-ROM.

Chris Bright, "Bio-Invasions: The Spread of Exotic Species," *World Watch*, July/August 1995. SIRS Knowledge Source. sks.sirs.com.

Patricia Leigh Brown, "The Plague of New Orleans," *New York Times*, May 14, 2000. www.nytimes.com/learning/students/pop/051400sci-animal-termite.html.

Pam Calvert, "Out of Control!: The Brown Tree Snake," *Odyssey*, April 2000. Cobblestone Publishing. www.cobblestonepub.com/pages/Oddpeek.html.

Dana Cole, "California's Urbanizing Wetlands and 'The Fire of the Future,'" Information Center for the Environment. www.ice.ucdavis.edu/cafe/agenda97/FireManagement/Planning/8FMCole.html.

Daniel Defoe, *A Journal of the Plague Year*, Classical Authors Directory. authorsdirectory.com/b/jplag10.htm.

Keith S. Delaplane, "Pesticide Usage in the United States: History, Benefits, Risks, and Trends," University of Georgia College of Agricultural & Environmental Services. www.ces.uga.edu/pubcd/B1121.htm.

Jack Doyle, *Altered Harvest*. New York: Viking Press, 1985. Unsafe Science. www.un-safescience.com/cms-sclb.html.

Food & Agriculture Organization, "Foodcrops & Shortages: Samoa," October 2000. www.fao.org/giews/english/fs/fs0010/pays/sam0010e.htm.

Patricia Gadsby, "Fear of Flu," *Discover*, January 1999. SIRS Knowledge Source. sks.sirs.com.

Steve Grant, "A Bug's Lifeline," *Hartford Courant*, September 14, 1999. SIRS Knowledge Source. sks.sirs.com.

International Plant Genetic Resources Institute, "TaroGen: Improving Nutrition and Incomes Through Taro Research," PGR-2, June 2000. www.ipgri.cgiar.org/pgr/pgr.asp?nb=2.

Dr. E. L. Skip Knox, "The Black Death," *ORB* (*The Online Reference Book for Medieval Studies*). orb.rhodes.edu/textbooks/westciv/blackdeath.html.

Kathleen McAuliffe, "The Killing Fields: Latter-Day Plagues," *Omni*, May 1990. SIRS Knowledge Source. sks.sirs.com.

Johanna McGeary, "Death Stalks a Continent," *Time*, February 12, 2001. www.time.com.

Joe Miller, "The Birds," *PitchWeekly Online*, October 26, 2000. pitch.com/issues/2000-10-26.stline.html.

National Fire Protection Association, "The Oakland/Berkeley Hills Fire of 1991." www.firewise.org/pubs/theOaklandBerkeleyHills Fire/abstract.html.

Nevard Family Website, "Eyewitness Accounts of Locust-Swarms." members.tripod.com/~NevFam2/material/locust.htm.

Shelly Parer, "History of the European Wild Rabbit in Australia." rubens.anu.edu.au/student.projects/rabbits/history. html.

Chris Reuther, "Invaders from Earth," Academy of Natural Sciences, May 1999. www.acnatsci.org/erd/ea/exotics.html.

Andrew C. Revkin, "March of the Fire Ants," *Discover*, March 1989. SIRS Knowledge Source. sks.sirs.com.

John Seewer, "Swarm of Annoyance: Lake Erie Insects Arrive," *Cincinnati Enquirer*, July 3, 2000. enquirer.com/editions/2000/07/03/loc_swarm_of_annoyance.html.

Daniel Simberloff, "Impacts of Introduced Species in the United States," *Consequences,* vol. 2, no. 2, 1996. U.S. Global Change Research Information Office. www.gcrio.org/CONSEQUENCES/vol2no2/article2.html.

UNAIDS, "Best Practice Summary Booklet: Introduction to Antiretroviral Therapy." www.unaids.org/bestpractice/collection/subject/care/antiretroviral.html.

Uncredited author, "Deaths by Starvation," *Cork Examiner,* February 1, 1847. View of the Famine. vassun.vassar.edu/~sttaylor/FAMINE/Examiner/Archives/Feb1847.html.

Uncredited author, "Emigration," *Cork Examiner*, April 5, 1847. View of the Famine. vassun.vassar.edu/~sttaylor/FAMINE/Examiner/Archives/Apr1847.html.

Uncredited author, "Sufferings of Emigrants in New York," *New York Sun*, May 19, 1847. View of the Famine. vassun.vassar.edu/~sttaylor/FAMINE/Examiner/Archives/May 1847.html

Bret Wallach, *At Odds with Progress: Americans and Conservation.* Tucson: University of Arizona Press, 1991. University of Oklahoma Geography Department's website.geography.ou.edu/research/aowp2.html.

Zai Whitaker, "Winning the Rat Race in India," *International Wildlife*, November/December 1992. SIRS Knowledge Source. sks.sirs.com.

Ron Wild, "The Black Death," *History Magazine*, October/November 1999. www.history-magazine.com/black.html.

World Health Organization, "Achievements and Challenges." www.who.int/aboutwho/en/achievements.html.

World Health Organization, "Tuberculosis Fact Sheet." www.who/int/inf-fs/en/fact104.html.

Periodicals
Sue Hubbell, "In Missouri: The Cicada's Song," *Time*, July 15, 1985.

National Science and Technology Council Committee on Environment and Natural Resources, "National Assessment of Harmful Algal Blooms in U.S. Waters," October 2000.

Ohio Lake Erie Commission, "101 Uses for a Mayfly?" *North Coast Newsletter*, September/October 2000.

U.S. Office of Technology Assessment, "Harmful Non-Indigenous Species in the United States," September 1993.

U.S. Office of Technology Assessment, "A Plague of Locusts," June 1990.

World Health Organization, "WHO Report on Global Surveillance of Epidemic-Prone Infectious Diseases," 2000.

Websites

UNAIDS (www.unaids.org). Describes the history, goals, and activities of the world's primary AIDS-action organization. Also includes information about the status of AIDS today.

World Health Organization (www.who.int). This extremely comprehensive website chronicles the activities and research of the WHO.

Index

Picture Credits

Cover photo: A. Crump, TDR, WHO/Science Photo Library/Photo Researchers, Inc.

© AFP/CORBIS, 22, 75

Agricultural Research Service, USDA, 11, 82, 91

AP Photo/Rob Griffith, 58

AP Photo/Handout, University of Florida, Thomas Wright, 47

AP Photo/Joe Marquette, 26

© Tony Arruza/CORBIS, 71

© Tiziana and Gianni Baldizzone/CORBIS, 89

© Tom Bean/CORBIS, 72

© Bettmann/CORBIS, 51, 63, 80, 83

© Nigel Cattlin/Holt Studios International/Photo Researchers, Inc., 35

© CORBIS, 49, 67

© Eye Ubiquitous/CORBIS, 77

© Michael Freeman/CORBIS, 44

© Chris Hellier/CORBIS, 56

© Historical Picture Archive/CORBIS, 29

© Hulton/Archive by Getty Images, 19, 31, 65

© Hulton-Deutsch Collection/CORBIS, 87

© George Kleiman/Photo Researchers, Inc., 38

Library of Congress, 13, 15, 20

Astrid & Hanns-Frieder Michler/Science Photo Library/Photo Researchers, Inc., 68

© Newman & Flowers/Photo Researchers, Inc., 53

© Gianni Dagli Orti/CORBIS, 9

© Papilio/CORBIS, 40

Photo by Corinne Dufka/Reuters, 25

© Roger Ressmeyer/CORBIS, 23

© Reuters NewMedia Inc./CORBIS, 85

© James H. Robinson/Photo Researchers, Inc., 41, 55

© Gianni Tortoli/Photo Researchers, Inc., 33

About the Author

Kris Hirschmann has written more than fifty books for children, mostly on science and nature topics. She is the author of *Hurricanes*, published by Lucent Books, and *Lions*, published by KidHaven Press.

Hirschmann is a freelance writer and a member of the Society of Children's Book Writers and Illustrators. She is also the president of The Wordshop, a business that provides a wide variety of writing and editorial services. She holds a bachelor's degree in psychology from Dartmouth College in Hanover, New Hampshire.

Hirschmann lives just outside of Orlando, Florida, with her husband, Michael.